Come Unto Me

Come
Unto
Me

*Rethinking
the Sacraments
for Children*

Elizabeth Francis Caldwell

UNITED CHURCH PRESS CLEVELAND, OHIO

United Church Press, Cleveland, Ohio 44115
© 1996 by Elizabeth Francis Caldwell

Printed in the United States of America on acid-free paper
01 00 99   5 4 3 2

Library of Congress Cataloging-in-Publication Data

Caldwell, Elizabeth, 1948–
Come unto me : rethinking the sacraments for children /
Elizabeth Francis Caldwell.
p.   cm.
Includes bibliographical references.
ISBN 0-8298-1119-2 (alk. paper)
1. Sacraments.   2. Christian education of children.   3. Children—Religious life.
4. Church work with children.   I. Title.
BV800.C34   1996
265'.082—dc20   95-51064
CIP

Contents

Acknowledgments

During my second year of teaching at McCormick Theological Seminary, I sat in on a theology class on the sacraments. I left that class to teach a new class I had designed, "Nurturing a People—Baptism through Confirmation." It was in the meeting of these two classes—the first focusing on the sacraments from a theological and liturgical perspective, and the second focusing on them from an educational perspective—that the passion for writing this book was born.

This book could not have been written without conversations with colleagues Deborah Mullen, Deborah Block, and Cynthia Campbell, whose thoughts on the sacraments in the life of a congregation have been invaluable. I am equally grateful for the participation and enthusiasm of many seminary students over the past eleven years. Thanks also to Nona Holy, John Wilkinson, Tracy Hindman, Donna Birney, Mark Hindman, and Renae McKee-Parker for the faithful ways they live in response to their baptisms and for allowing me to share their stories.

I appreciate the work of my editor, Kim Sadler, and her interest in and commitment to this project. I am also thankful for the members of my family, who have patiently listened and provided helpful critiques as my thinking has evolved. Conversations with my sister, Cathy, have been of special importance whenever I have written about children and faith, an issue she deals with on a daily basis.

I dedicate this book with grateful appreciation and love to the children of faith who teach me about God's love and care for all creation: Josh, Russell, and Christopher Hoop, and Mary Elizabeth and Andrew James Caldwell.

1 Faith Nurturing: Whose Responsibility?

Josh was three when his family decided to sell their house and look for a new place to live. His mother began to prepare him for this change; she told him they would soon leave their house for another one. Josh told her he loved the house they lived in and didn't want to move. She patiently explained that people live in different places during their life, and one day he would grow up and have his own place to live. This particular concept was one that Josh was not ready to accept. "Mommy, I want to live with you when I grow up. I don't want to live by myself. I would need someone to love me."

Josh was affirming his love and trust as well as a basic human need—to love and be loved. And just as Josh's mother suggests that his family will not always be the main source of this love, I will suggest in this book that the home and the church must work as partners in providing the love and nurture that is the foundation for growing in the Christian faith. Unfortunately, this relationship is often one-sided. Some parents expect the church to teach their children everything they need to know about the Christian faith, while they miss daily opportunities to live that faith with their children. Some congregations exclude children from worship and other vital ministries, thus making clear their understanding of who is welcome in the community of faith.

Jesus' invitation to the children to "come unto me" must be reexamined by congregations today. A church's programs of education and patterns of worship illustrate how Jesus' invitation is valued in the life of that congregation.

1

In this chapter I will challenge some of the familiar ways we conceptualize and engage in the activity of faith nurturing, and I will raise questions about participation in and ownership of this responsibility we all share as members of the body of Christ. I will define *faith nurturing* in very simple terms: loving and living faithfully with our children and young people.

Hulda Niebuhr was a professor of Christian education at McCormick Theological Seminary from 1945 to 1959. One of the items found in her papers was a book of poems written and collected over several years and given to her mother as a Christmas gift in 1929. The following poem provides a way to begin thinking about faith nurturing.

Warm Little Frictions

This strange city is so cold—
Everyone speaks so smoothly to me.
What a comfort they were,
The "warm little frictions of home!"

At home
Someone would have told me
That I had let my shoulders
Become stooped,
That my opinions on the state of the universe
Need some amendments;
And I must practice more, for my last solo
Was not my best;
That my new hat, so proudly worn
Was not too wisely chosen.

But here,
No one loves me enough
To take the twinkle to disagree
With me;
No one cares sufficiently
To take the chance
Of hurting me:
"How perfectly lovely!"
"How absolutely correct!"

I did not know what a comfort they were,
The "warm little frictions of home."
And how chilly it would be
Away from the love that is their source.[1]

The contrast in the poem is between the intimate knowledge and honest love inherent in the "warm frictions" of the home and the cool detachment and anonymity of life outside of that household. For Hulda Niebuhr, home was a place of warmth, honesty, and occasional disagreement, all in an atmosphere of love and trust.

A Commitment to Faith Formation

Household frictions must be our goal if we are to live out a commitment to faith forming, so that what we believe and what we confess and affirm are not truly understood until they are acted upon in the world.

To reach this goal, we first must reexamine the metaphor of the church as family. Perhaps this metaphor is so widely used because churches find it comfortable and descriptive of what they are trying to be—a place to support people's growth in faith, enabling the translation of faith into ethical Christian living. I once saw a poster saying the best things we can give our children are roots and wings—a grounding in tradition and the encouragement to challenge dominant ideologies and seek new ways of seeing, being, and acting in a world working to bring about God's justice and peace. Most churches would say they are trying to give their members—their children—these very things.

Unfortunately, churches that see themselves as families have at times done a poor job of giving roots and wings. Rather than working to create a space for grace for all people, such churches have sometimes legitimated practices that have both implicitly and explicitly communicated different goals.

For example, churches sometimes communicate antithetical understandings of evangelism. We want more members, we need young people, we say, while at the same time we fail to nurture the people we have, especially the youngest ones in our midst. Often our commitments to stewardship, mission, and pastoral care are a matter of church size or participant age. Many congregations exclude or ignore children and youth in congregational worship.

Such congregational practices indicate frictions within the household of faith. It is time to examine these practices and introduce some
dissonance into the familiar metaphor of the church as family.[2]

A Shift in Metaphors: The Household of God

Janet Fishburn and Letty Russell are two educators and theologians
who are providing just such counterpressure. In her book *Confronting
the Idolatry of the Family: A New Vision for the Household of God,*
Fishburn suggests *household* as an alternative metaphor to *family pew,*
which she believes empowers "the domestic captivity of the church."[3]

The metaphor of the church as family pew, she believes, has do-
mesticated the Christian faith to the extent that members are not required to know, be, or do anything any differently from those who
participate in any community volunteer organization. Fishburn boldly
states the obvious when she says that for most church members, "the
Christian home has not functioned as a center for family Bible study
for well over a century."[4] Yet we still believe the home to be a partner
with the congregation in the responsibility for passing on the faith.
This assumption, says Fishburn, is foolish.

If baptism, communion, and confirmation are matters of family
tradition rather than faithful responses within God's household, they
become, she says, "associated with the family life cycle," rituals that
are "only rites of passage for 'birthright Christians' who 'prefer to
grow their own' new members."[5] And so we see parents insisting their
children attend confirmation class at age fourteen because that's when
they did it. If the young person protests, such parents often promise
that if the youth attends the class and gets confirmed, they won't make
him or her go to church anymore.

The metaphor of church as household of God (Eph. 2:16) offers a
vision of congregational life as a space for grace, where in worship, in
study, in the integration of faith and life, the forming of faith enables
transformation (Eph. 4:15).

While Fishburn's metaphor is used to challenge traditional assumptions about the relationship of family and church from an educational and liturgical perspective, Letty Russell uses the metaphor
household of freedom to critique ecclesiological authority. According

to Russell, a household of freedom (as described in Galatians) is a "community of mutual caring," where partnership is valued and practiced.[6] For example, postresurrection Christian communities had their meetings in households. Long-held patriarchal and hierarchical relationships were replaced with ones of equality (1 Cor. 1:26–30).

Both Fishburn and Russell, I believe, are advocating dissonance and challenging dominant metaphors to help us see the church as a space for transformation, a space for God's grace and God's challenge.

Integrating Education and Worship

We need friction! We need to become "household revolutionaries," according to Letty Russell. Or, says Mary Hunt in the book *Women and Church: The Challenge of Ecumenical Solidarity in an Age of Alienation,* we need to become "ecclesial termites."[7] Like termites on a wood porch, we need to eat away at the long-held ecclesiological, theological, and educational traditions and practices that do not affirm the relationship between the holy and the daily, between the vision and the reality of God's dominion in the world. It is essential that we integrate worship and education, and more particularly the sacraments and the life of the people in the household of faith.

We set an open table, but we have reserved seating. The meal is served to adults, but often not to children.

Some ask, "Why can't those children be baptized in a special service so it doesn't disrupt our Sunday worship?" Others believe that if we have church school at the same time as worship, then children won't interrupt the service.

We are the inheritors of a sacramental tradition that is often unwelcoming, cognitively based, individually focused, separated from religious education, divorced from the practice of faith, and tied as much to social traditions as to theological affirmations.

We separate life from worship, worship from the sacraments; the sacraments thus become twice removed from life. What should be life giving, life forming, has become sterile, routine, unfeeling, almost as if we are threatened to come to God and unable to look one another in the eye. We make ourselves religious paupers, isolated and alienated from one another, from the world, and from God.

This grim assessment does not have to be a continuing reality. We are also the inheritors of a rich and colorful religious tradition (Deut. 6:4., Matt. 22:34–40, 1 Pet. 2:9).

Rebuilding the Household

Russell suggests that as revolutionaries, we have three tools for rebuilding the household.

First, we need to be hospitable to all persons in the household of God. A simple and fairly obvious beginning is to recognize the worth and value of all persons in God's household of freedom. Everyone has a name and likes to be called by that name, especially children. Who do we call by name and welcome into our midst? Does our hospitality extend even to the stranger among us?

Congregations welcome families with children because they know it means the church school will grow. There is the implicit understanding that a congregation with a growing nursery and active programs for children is more attractive to parents. But are families with children welcome as a unit, or only as they separate according to ages?

The practice of many congregations regarding times for worship and times for religious education stands in sharp contrast to the initial word of welcome made to families with children. In other words, many congregations have church school at the same time as worship. In this model, children and youth are present in worship for only a short time or not at all. Such a practice excludes children and youth from participating in or leading congregational worship, and most adults do not have the opportunity to be a part of their religious education.

The question of who is invited and welcomed to congregational worship is related to theological, ecclesiological, developmental, and cultural understandings and practices. What is worship? Who can worship? Is worship related to awe, reverence, quiet, order, tradition, stillness, and dress code? Or is it related to expression, preparation, response, color, sounds, music, taste, smell, noise, and movement?

Second, Russell says we must listen to the underside, to those who "live by hope, not by nostalgia." This means we must listen to children and youth when they ask the following questions:

"Why do I have to join the church? I thought I was already a part of it."

"Why can't I eat that bread and drink that juice?"

"Mommy, what are they doing to the baby? I can't see."

"Why is everyone so sad during communion, Dad?"

Some congregations participate in only one infant baptism service a year. Other congregations have the joy of experiencing an infant baptism as frequently as once a month. In what ways does this sacramental moment affect the family and the family of faith? Is it something to be done early in the service so the baby won't disturb worship? Are infant baptisms understood as a time for all people in the worshiping community to consider and renew their baptismal vows, or are they considered interruptions of the "regular" service, making the service of worship last too long?

Is participation at Christ's Table, eating the meal in memory and celebration of Jesus Christ, a matter of knowledge, age, and maturity? Or is sharing the bread and the cup an act of living and growing in faith, an act of membership in God's household?

What about the so-called in-between time, that period of time between an infant's baptism and a young adult's confirmation of faith and commissioning as a member of a congregation? Have young adults had sufficient nurture and experiences in worship, stewardship, and mission to know that the church is a place they want to be, that their faith is truly theirs?

Ministers Stuart Smith and Peter Brick work for the Night Ministry, a program reaching out to homeless youth and adults on the streets of Chicago. In their conversations with some of the four thousand homeless young people in that city, they have discovered that most of these youth are baptized Christians. How did these children come to be unwanted, unloved, and forgotten? When and how do we hear their voices?

In his book *The Spiritual Life of Children,* Robert Coles shares his conversations with children about their faith, stories accumulated from years of listening. While he wrote this book, Anna Freud suggested that Coles should "let the children help you with their ideas on the subject."[8] He discovered that the children were "seekers" attempting to make sense of their world and their faith, much like the rest of us.

We need to become better listeners, focusing on *catechesis,* which means, literally, "echoing down." Through *education*—from the Latin "leading forth"—catechesis can become less a process of memorizing questions and answers and more a dialogue as children, youth, and adults, in a partnership of learning, echo down the faith, leading each other forth to new understandings of what it means to live faithfully in response to God's call.

And third, Russell believes that an essential tool for rebuilding a household of freedom is to live with imagination. This has three implications.

Educationally, living with imagination means that we remember children's baptisms by retelling the baptism story and sending them baptism cards each year (or by making a baptismal wall in which a nameplate for each child lists their baptism date and includes a space to add the date of their confirmation, as the Presbyterian Church of Western Springs, Illinois, has done).

Living with imagination calls for us to view worship space from the viewpoint of education. Is this space welcoming of children and conducive to their participation? It also means we expect parents to think about and discuss the sacraments with their children prior to those important events.

Congregations need new lenses with which to view their practices of stewardship, mission, and pastoral care. Who is encouraged to be a steward—a three-year-old child as well as a forty-five-year-old adult? Who is asked to help prepare a meal for a shut-in or a homeless person—a child or a teenager as well as an adult? Who gets a pastoral call during a time of family crisis—only the adults, or the children and teenagers as well?

As for our programs of Christian education, we have become curriculum dependent. Denominational curricula are both a bane and a blessing. Age-appropriate curricula with practical teaching suggestions are an incredible asset. The resources of editors, educators, scholars, and theologians can help us think holistically about the content, process, and application of our faith.

But when no curriculum is available, we often don't know what to do, how to plan, design, and implement an effective program of study. User friendly has led to user dependent. How can we rescue our creative, storytelling capabilities from extinction? How can we become faithful persons capable of passing on the biblical story to new generations, capable of nurturing even the youngest ones in our midst as they ask questions about their faith and their world?

Theologically, living with imagination means engaging in sacramental education. Communion is rarely joyful. Baptisms seldom afford the opportunity for the congregation to remember and renew their baptismal vows. What if the water and the meal were joined so that children's welcome into the household of God affirmed their full participation? Having been washed and fed, they would be ready to grow in a life of faith supported by the witness and example of each member of God's household. Their presence at the table could not be denied.

Living with imagination means we take seriously our role as theologians. We are a people of faith. We know and live out a Christian faith tradition that we have both inherited and claimed as our own. Such a faith tradition needs nurturing in order to grow. Church school takes place once a week for some thirty to sixty minutes, but what is taught during that time must be discussed, interpreted, and reflected upon in the intervening days from Sunday to Sunday.

The home as a center of living and learning about the faith is essential in nurturing Christian lives. What is the core of such a faithful home—prayer, readings from the Bible, reflection at the end of the day, acts of service and kindness to others? What are we doing to support parents in their role as faith nurturers?

Liturgically, living with imagination implies that worship space is truly holy space where all the senses are involved, so that worship becomes an experience of the whole self in community, a activity in which persons of all ages are welcome. What if the bread came forth from the congregation lovingly offered by small hands, strong hands, even hands that are not quite as steady as they once were?

What if the water were poured so we could all see it?

What if we had to look at each other and call each other by name at the table?

What if during a baptism, children and any shorter adults who desired could sit in the front row (which no one else seems to want, anyway). Then they could see that in which they are participants.

What if children were the first to greet the newest one in their midst, perhaps even with a drop of oil gently placed on the one being baptized?

Household Frictions as Catalyst

As ecclesial termites, we can begin to raise such questions while we continue to offer hospitality, listen to the underside, and work to imagine what might be possible. Household frictions can serve as a catalyst for the transformation of people, families, and congregations as we move into the world in faithful response to God.

Josh, the boy we met at the beginning of this chapter, did not want to face the changes in his life. Having no experience of what a move to a new house would mean, he needed assurance that the changes in his world would be accompanied by the certainty of love.

To leave the assurance and certainty of the known and move into the unknown—raising questions, struggling to identify reality, and then living with the "warm little frictions of home"—requires going out in faith, hope, and trust. But to truly nurture the faith of all God's children, we must begin to live into some difficult questions and form visions of new possibilities.

2 Pouring the Water

Families await the birth or adoption of a child with excitement, joy, and perhaps some fear. Questions about parenthood are always in the back of the mind. Are we prepared? What if we don't know what to do? Where do we go for help? What kind of child will this be? What kind of parent will I be? Will I have enough patience to be with this child, to hear the questions and struggle with the answers? Will this child be healthy and happy?

These same questions remain throughout a child's life. Questions about faith also arise. Are we prepared to share our faith with this child? How do I live my faith so that what I believe is consistent with my words and actions? Where do we go for help with our concerns? What about my faith? What do I really believe? What if we don't know how to answer our child's questions—what do we say? What kind of Christian parent will I be? Will our life as a family be different because of our faith? In what ways will this congregation support us in our commitment to tell the biblical story to this child and to live our lives as Christians in this world?

If these questions have not arisen before a child's baptism, they certainly will surface then. The questions asked of parents and the affirmations made by congregations during a baptism require thoughtful preparation and intentional responses. Addressing the issue of accountability and intentionality on the part of parents and congregations, Gail Ramshaw says this:

> There is great pastoral responsibility to see that the households of
> baptized children have some understanding of what baptism is and
> that they commit themselves to raising the child in the faith. The

> Church will have a difficult job preaching the centrality of baptism
> if in practice baptism is automatically available on a moment's no-
> tice to anyone remotely connected with the church.[1]

Just as the birth or adoption of a child forever changes a family, infant baptism forever changes a congregation. In her book *Confronting
the Idolatry of Family, A New Vision for the Household of God,* Janet
Fishburn says the following:

> If infant baptism, the confirmation of baptismal vows, and new
> member rituals do not require a potential 'member' to know, do, or
> be anything in particular, no one should be surprised that congrega-
> tions lack spiritual vitality. If these rituals require no clear commit-
> ment to regular worship, disciplined study, and participation in
> ministry by members, then there is little reason to expect church
> members to be different from the members of any other voluntary
> organization.[2]

If the sacrament of baptism is to be more than just a social ritual—
the moment in worship when we hurry the family in and "do the
baby"—then it is essential to consider the following questions:

1. What beliefs and meanings contribute to our understanding and
   experience of the sacrament of baptism?
2. Who is a baptism for?
3. What is the role of the congregation in preparing a family for a
   child's baptism?
4. What educational and liturgical models enable a renewed understanding of this sacrament in the life of a family and a congregation?

Baptism starts the journey in understanding the hallowed name of
God.[3] All Christians are involved in this journey, not just the family of
the baptized one. This chapter addresses the issue of faith forming and
the role of parents and congregations as partners in this process. It affirms the integrative relationship between Christian education and
worship and the role of infant baptism in the growing faith of children,
their families, and their congregations.

The following story helps identify the educational and liturgical
aspects of the sacrament of baptism. As you read the story, make notes

in the margin about issues you identify as essential to your understanding of baptism.

Baptism Day

It was Palm Sunday, the Sabbath day marking the end of Lent and the beginning of Holy Week. It was also a day of baptism for two brothers, one age three and the other nine months. The week before the baptism, the older child was taken by his mother into the sanctuary to see the font. She explained to him what was going to happen at his baptism. His main concern was that the water be cool, not hot. She assured him that it would be cool.

The awaited day arrived. Family members and friends had traveled from many places to join the congregation gathered for a Palm Sunday celebration. The service began with children bringing down the representation of the sacraments—the bread and the cup. The lay liturgist for this Sunday, a member of the confirmation class, carried the pitcher with the water. All were carefully placed on the communion table. Green palm branches were in abundance for all to wave as the service began with singing.

At the start of the liturgy of the baptism, the parents came forward with their children. The three year old really wanted to bring along his blanket but decided it was all right for his grandmother to hold it for him. The nine month old was not going to be so easily parted from his much loved teddy bear. As the minister began to address faith questions to the parents, she remembered another baptism day twenty-nine years earlier, the baptism of the mother of these two children. The same questions had been asked, the public statement of faith had been made, the promises to help the child grow in her Christian faith had been affirmed by her family and the congregation. And now this woman and her husband were living out their baptismal promises and bringing forth their children to be welcomed by a community of faith gathered in worship.

The minister talked through her emotions and her memories and took the children from her sister and brother-in-law. The older child climbed onto a stool and helped to pour the living water into the font. These children of God, children of the covenant that God made so long ago with God's people, were welcomed with water into a believing and

loving community of faith. With the parents, the congregation said to-
gether its affirmation of faith, the Apostles' Creed. Prayers for this
particular family and this congregation concluded the baptismal
liturgy on a beautiful spring day.

Family pictures were taken around the font before going home to a
festive lunch. Baptismal gifts were opened—a Bible storybook, a
Noah's ark puzzle, and a book about baptism. Everyone enjoyed the
food, the conversation, the children, and the storytelling.

The story of this day has been remembered and retold with words
and pictures. When the newest member of the family was baptized,
three baptismal candles were lit at the lunch after the baptism. The
baby was lovingly passed among family and friends as they all ate,
visited, and told stories. Pictures were taken to add to the family book
of baptisms. This handmade book, a gift on the first occasion, was
brought out once again to be touched and read.

Beliefs and Meanings

Implicit in this baptism story are a number of explicit beliefs and
meanings essential to an understanding of baptism. Before examining
these meanings, first consider your own definition of and experience
with baptism. Take a few minutes here to complete this statement:
Baptism is . . .

Baptisms are occasions when families come together. At such occasions, family members both remember past events and look forward
to the life of promise that the child represents. Congregations do the
same thing at this moment of welcome. In his book *Worship*, John
Burkhart says the following:

> Baptizing is something done to someone . . . a welcome through wa-
> ter . . . a public event.
>   Being baptized is the beginning of a process of ministry.
>   Baptism is that gracious activity in which those who are being
> saved to serve are "added" to an assembly that gathers, celebrates
> time, shares feasts and serves.
>   Baptism is the beginning.
>   To baptize or to be baptized:
>   • acknowledges that we live our lives in a God-given history.

- rehearses life as it is meant to be, full of promise, enriched with vital memories, and open to the future.
- proclaims that all our lives are planted in grace and constituted by promises.[4]

For baptism to take place, parents must make a faith decision for themselves and for their child. Baptism means that they are intentionally and publicly proclaiming their faith in God, the saving work of the Savior, and the abiding presence of the Spirit in their life. In *Alternative Futures for Worship,* Mark Searle says that baptism "is the deliberate and conscious insertion of the child into the environment of faith, which faith is the faith of the Church, which in turn is the faith of Christ himself."[5]

The faith of the parents is intimately connected to the faith of the child presented for baptism. The sacrament is not a one-time event. Rather, it is a life-forming and life-connecting faith event. Two Christian denominations have made this connection explicit in their statements about the sacrament. In the *Book of Worship,* the United Church of Christ states that by baptism, "a person becomes a member of Christ's church and is welcome at Christ's table. For the newly baptized, the journey is from font to the feast of the table."[6] In *The Directory for Worship,* the Presbyterian Church (U.S.A.) states the following:

> Baptism is the sign and seal of incorporation into Christ.
> Baptism enacts and seals what the Word proclaims: God's redeeming grace offered to all people.
> Baptism is God's gift of grace and also God's summons to respond to that grace.
> The baptism of children witnesses to the truth that God's love claims people before they are able to respond in faith.[7]

Baptism takes place in a public worship service, not a private christening service, because we believe that the congregation must welcome the child and promise to be involved in nurturing the child's faith and supporting the family. Robert Browning and Roy Reed claim that the "sacrament of baptism is a public celebration of God's unconditional love of the child and an engrafting of the infant into the family of Christ, making the child a full member of Christ's body, the church."[8]

On the occasion of a baptism, family and friends often travel great distances to come together in the household of faith where the child will grow and be nurtured. On this sacramental day, a child is welcomed and the congregation is renewed. Janet Fishburn reminds us of the power of this sacrament in the lives of all those gathered for worship:

> When observed with regularity, the celebration of the sacraments can be a time of renewal, a time that marks new movements in the life of faith. As visible signs of God's love and forgiveness, baptism and the Supper can extend the horizons of believers from limited visions of the church as local and particular toward a sense that they belong to the whole communion of saints. The baptismal water, the bread and the cup, are present reminders that Christians are called out, cleansed, and constantly renewed as they participate in the eternal love of God through their membership in the Body of Christ.[9]

A baptism reminds a congregation that they have changed. A new child has been welcomed and blessed, anointed with water and commissioned for a life of faith. The congregation must have a clear sense of how they will welcome this child's presence and potential leadership among them. Browning and Reed state that infant baptism "is much more than the giving of a new status. It is a commissioning for participation in the ministering community. It is an ordination of the child into the universal priesthood. And, as any parent knows, the spontaneous life of the child quickly ministers unto us as much as we minister unto the child."[10]

When a family comes together after a baptism, the gathering of grandparents, aunts and uncles, family friends, and church members is a visible sign of connection across the ages with God's church and with each other. The "Baptism, Eucharist, and Ministry" document of the World Council of Churches affirms this connection when it says that baptism "is the sign of new life through Jesus Christ. It unites the one baptized with Christ and with his people. . . . Baptism is a sign and seal of our common discipleship. Through baptism, Christians are brought into union with Christ, with each other and with the Church of every time and place. Baptism is both God's gift and our human response to that gift. It looks towards a growth into the measure of the stature of the fullness of Christ (Eph. 4:13)."[11]

Now, look again at your own definition of baptism in light of the statements in the preceding paragraphs. What concepts are most important in your definition? Our discussion so far has suggested six concepts that serve as the foundation for our beliefs about the sacrament of baptism:

1. Baptism is *grounded in biblical understandings* of the significance of water in the story of God's relationship with God's people. Baptisms connect us deeply with the New Testament stories of Jesus being baptized and baptizing. As with the sacrament of communion, baptism follows a biblical example. Baptismal images of beginnings, preparation, vocation, and unity all have their basis in biblical passages.

2. Baptism as a sacrament of the church is both a *sign* of the presence of God in the life of the church and a *symbol* of God's action in our world. This sacrament reminds us who we are and who God is calling us to be—God's children. The waters of baptism mark us for a life of faithful service and witness in God's name.

   In her book for children *Signs of God's Love: Baptism and Communion,* Jeanne Fogle reminds us of the meaning of this symbol: "Our baptism is the sign that we belong to God and to the whole family of Christians everywhere."[12]

3. Explicit in the preceding discussion is the idea that baptism is an *action that takes place in worship.* In baptism, a new life is brought into a worshiping community, and as Burkhart affirms, "No community is ever the same after it has been invaded by the new."[13] In baptism, a child is named and claimed. "Child of the covenant, I baptize you in the name of the God who loves you, the Redeemer who saves you, and the Spirit who gives you life."[14]

4. The baptismal liturgy provides opportunity for both *affirmation* and *promise*. Parents profess their faith in Jesus Christ, and with the congregation they promise to nurture their child in the Christian faith. Members of the congregation then have the opportunity to join in partnership with the family in nurturing the child. "Do you as members of the church of Jesus Christ, promise to guide and nurture [this child] by word and deed, with

love and prayer, encouraging them to know and follow Christ and to be faithful members of his church?"[15] "Do you, who witness and celebrate this sacrament, promise your love, support, and care to the one about to be baptized, as she/he lives and grows in Christ?"[16]

5. The act of welcome with water is both a *gift* and a *response*. We baptize with water as a reminder of God's covenantal promises made long ago; God's gift of life and love are visibly enacted at a baptism. The ways that families and congregations nurture children in the Christian faith affirms our response to this gift.

6. The baptismal act is a public affirmation that the *process* of a life of faith has begun, a new life called by God in *unity* with Christians in every time and place. Baptism affirms God's call and commission for ministry in the world. The act of baptizing forever unites the newest member to the sacrament of communion.

Who Is Baptism For?

This question might sound simplistic at first, but asking it reveals a number of assumptions that must be made explicit if our practice of this sacrament is to have biblical, theological, and liturgical integrity. It is likely that a range of understandings and intentions regarding infant baptism exists within a congregation. Consider these:

- Children must be baptized as soon after birth as possible so that their sins are forgiven.
- My grandchild is coming for a visit and I want him baptized in my church because his parents won't do it. I want my grandchild to grow up knowing Jesus.
- Baptizing my child is what I'm expected to do. My parents did it for me, so I need to bring my child for infant baptism.
- We want as many of our family and friends as possible to be here for our daughter's baptism.

Searle suggests that "most modern Christians have inherited a drastically impoverished understanding of the wealth and wonder of the baptismal life. . . . A newly baptized child is not merely one who is delivered from sin and from the threat of damnation, but one claimed by the irrescindable Word of God to be an adopted child of God, a living member of Christ, a temple of the Holy Spirit."[17] The impoverishment Searle mentions is in part the result of cultural and familial traditions dominating sacramental and liturgical practices. But clergy have also played a role in this impoverishment. For example, some clergy place the baptism early in the service so that they can get the baby out before it cries. Still others plan separate services for infant baptisms so as not to take time away from regular worship.

Families that baptize their children because baptism is a social ritual, a part of their family tradition, or a way to assure them in their own faith demonstrate the problems that arise with what Fishburn calls the "automatic availability" of the sacrament. How can a congregation affirm their promise of Christian nurture if the child lives in another city and is being baptized for the grandparents?

An honest no to parents who have no intention of bringing their child to church or of actively nurturing their child's growth in faith is a better answer than water automatically available at a moment's notice. A service of naming and blessing for a grandchild who lives in another city has more theological integrity than a baptism, which would ask a congregation to promise something they cannot do.

Congregations and families need to think intentionally about the commitment being made at a baptism. Some pastors and congregations have addressed this commitment when asked to baptize a child who attends another church—they have performed the baptism in partnership with the home congregation. On the Sunday of the baptism, the home congregation includes a prayer for the child and the family in its service of worship.

So just who is baptism for? It is for parents, their child, their congregation, and their family and friends, the entire household that has gathered for worship in faithful response to God's call. Instead of making baptismal water automatically available, we need to reconceptualize the sacrament in terms of its lifelong formative possibilities. Baptism has continuing consequences throughout a person's life.

Louis Gunnemann argues against a privatization of the Christian faith that focuses on "self-serving religious life." He asks, "Why does the church in these critical times continue this religious ritual which is not only often accompanied by mushy sentimentality but is also

among many people so little understood?"[18] Gunnemann challenges
us to think of baptism in terms of Christian vocation. Such a rethinking, he believes, moves the sacrament from the convenient periphery
to the center of the life, ministry, and mission of a congregation. I
agree with Gunnemann that "the liturgical and educational life of the
church must be organized around the full meaning and practice of
baptism."[19]

Gunnemann invites churches to reconceive the role of the family
and the congregation, moving from a commitment to the educational
process to a responsibility for the nurturing process.[20] His distinction
between the educational and nurturing processes is an important one.
Congregations take pride in the variety of programs they offer for the
Christian education of their children. But how seriously do most congregations take their role as partners with families in nurturing lives of
Christian vocation?

As you read through the rest of this chapter, keep in mind this distinction between education and nurture. As you study the suggested
congregational models, try to distinguish which are based in nurture,
and which in education.

The Congregation's Role in Preparing
Families for Baptism

Planning for infant baptisms is usually handled by a congregation's minister and the church office. Congregations with an informal
style of administration and planning usually have an implicit practice
of allowing the parents, working with the minister, to decide the appropriate time for infant baptism. Large congregations that must plan
for baptisms of large numbers of infants generally have a more explicitly stated process of coordinating baptisms on certain Sundays in the
liturgical calendar.

What seems to be missing is a holistic approach to baptism that involves preparing families for more than just the actual day of baptism.
The following story represents a composite of many stories I have
heard about congregational practices and parental hopes related to infant baptism. As you read it, consider the issues involved in imple-
menting a sacramental model of education and worship.

It Takes a Village[21]

Tom and Louise were very excited about the news of Louise's pregnancy. As they moved through the months of waiting, they began to think about parenthood. Already their lives were beginning to change. Doctor's appointments, hospital visits, birthing classes, and shopping for all the things needed for an infant filled up the time between work, home, and church commitments. They quickly realized that the impending birth of their child affected every aspect of their life together.

The same was true of another couple awaiting the arrival of a child. Luke and Diane's application for adoption had been completed for several years, and they had finally received word that a child had been found for them. They had delayed thinking about this reality until they knew it would actually happen. Their planning for the child's arrival had to take place quickly, since they didn't have nine months'notice.

Both of these families were members of the same congregation. After telling their extended families and close friends, the soon-to-be parents shared their news with their pastor and congregation. This family of faith took its baptismal vows seriously; they believed that the journey to birth and adoption was a partnership. The members of the congregation were prepared to wait with the two couples through education and liturgy.

The church's Christian Education Committee, working with the Worship Committee, had planned a cooperative approach to baptism that began as soon as they heard the news. They knew that the culture prepared parents for birth and adoption with all kinds of parenting classes, but they believed that their responsibility for Christian nurturing began with the expectant couples, helping them prepare, living with their faith questions, and journeying with them along the way to parenthood. They believed that the baptism of a child was more than one special day, that it should be celebrated in stages.[22] These stages included the anticipation and celebration of the birth or adoption itself as well as the anticipation and celebration of the actual baptism.

When the expectant couples were ready to share their news with the entire congregation, prayers for the safety and health of the mothers were offered in the prayers of the people during Sunday worship. The expecting families were visited by a member of the Christian Education Committee or by the pastor. They were given a booklet pre-

*pared by the church, titled "We Welcome Your Child." The booklet was
the work of several church committees and was made available to expectant parents as well as to church visitors with children. The booklet
contained sections entitled "Programs for Children," "Worshiping
with Your Child," "Nurturing Your Faith," "Living Your Faith with Your
Child," and "Resources in the Church Library."*

*This visit also included an invitation to the adults to attend a class
for prospective parents. The class, offered once a year, consisted of
four sessions during church school. It included a discussion of the
meaning of baptism, time to address any faith questions raised by the
participants, and a visit to the nursery and preschool classes. At
the conclusion, each family was given a copy of the book* Beginning a
Journey, *by Betty McLaney, and a first-year calendar for their child,*
Step by Step, *by Carol A. Wehrheim. (Both are published by the
Presbyterian Publishing House.)*

*Tom and Louise and Luke and Diane attended the four sessions to-
gether and enjoyed sharing their hopes, their fears, and their dreams.
A month after the last session, Luke and Diane received a call from
their adoption agency; they could take their child home. On the Sunday after the call, a rose in the sanctuary reminded the whole congregation that the family of faith was welcoming its newest child. A
member of the church took the rose and a loaf of bread and left them
with the new family that Sunday afternoon.*

*Tom and Louise's daughter was soon born, and she was welcomed
in the same way. In the months after this adoption and birth, the
friendship that had been formed between the two couples during their
time of waiting had became even stronger. The two families decided to
have their children baptized on the same Sunday. A week before the
baptism, the minister and other persons participating in the ceremony
met in the sanctuary with the pastor to go over the liturgy that would
be used.*

*The Worship Committee had prepared a small booklet, "The
Church's Welcome: The Sacrament of Baptism." This booklet had
evolved over many years of experience. The committee knew that for
many persons in the church, baptism was a special day, an important
sacrament in the ritual life of the congregation. They also knew that
others came to this sacrament for different reasons: social, familial, or
traditional. The intent of the booklet was to give parents a chance to*

*think about the sacrament ahead of time and reflect on the faith ques-
tions they would be asked.*

*The baptism day arrived. Friends and extended family were
warmly welcomed by the household of God. The liturgy for baptism in
this congregation included several traditions. Words were spoken,
promises were made and renewed, water was sprinkled, prayers were
offered, and God's assembly of the faithful welcomed again its newest
children.*

*After the service, everyone came forward to meet and greet the
children and the families. Pictures were taken and stories were
shared. Later that week, a member of the congregation who had participated in the baptism with the minister delivered a basket prepared
by the Christian Education and Worship Committees. It contained a
picture of the family taken after the baptism, a small plant, and a baptism card made by children in the church.*

*The children baptized that day had been welcomed before they
even entered the world. Their parents had been nurtured, sustained,
and supported in their journey to parenthood. The congregation was
ready to be a faithful village committed to raising children in the
Christian faith. In the children's book* It Takes a Village, *written and illustrated by Jane Cowen-Fletcher, Kokou and Yemi wandered off, and
when they returned home they thought their mother would be worried.
Mama wisely told them that even though they thought they had been
alone, they really were not, because "It takes a village to raise a child."*

Educational and Liturgical Models

This section presents four models that can be used in congregational
settings to enhance the experience of baptism. They are outlined in de-
tail to help you with your own thinking and planning.

1. "Nurturing a Life": A Class for Prospective Parents

This class includes four sessions that can be offered during church
school or in the evening, once a week for a month.

Purpose. The purpose of the class is to help parents think about
the ways they intend to nurture their child in the Christian faith, beginning with the public act of baptism. Preparing for this sacrament

involves thinking about faith—the faith of the child and the faith of the parents who will raise this child.

Objectives. By the end of the sessions, learners will have had the chance to do the following:

- Identify and discuss the biblical and theological meaning of the sacrament of infant baptism.
- Articulate questions and concerns about baptism and being faithful parents.
- Become familiar with child care options and children's classes available to the congregation.
- Rehearse together the liturgy for the sacrament of baptism.
- Become familiar with various resources for parents and for use with children.

Session One: "Baptism and Its Meanings"

Purpose. The purpose of this session is to discuss the meaning of baptism from a biblical, theological, denominational, congregational, and familial perspective.

Activities. One way to begin this session is to let the participants voice their questions about baptism or complete the statement "Baptism means. . . ." Another way to begin is to read stories of baptism from the New Testament.

A presentation on the six foundational beliefs about baptism taken from the "Beliefs and Meanings" section of this chapter could be a major part of this session. Check your denomination's resources for books or videos that might be useful.

Session Two: "Parenting for Faith Expression, Living Faithfully with Your Child"

Purpose. The purpose of this session is to consider the questions and concerns participants have about living the Christian faith with their child. It should include a discussion of some specific ways to parent for faith expression.

Activities. Some topics to include in this session are as follows:

- Praying for and with your child
- The faith of a preschool child
- Table blessings to say and sing

• Books to read (for yourself and with your child)
• Simple things to remember about faithful living
• Living as a steward of God's world
• Teaching children to take care of their bodies and take care of God's earth
• Dealing with issues of extended family
• Raising a child in a multifaith home

This session could be team-taught by an educator or pastor and a parent.

Session Three: "Caring for and Nurturing Your Child at Church"

Purpose. The purpose of this session is to familiarize new parents with the child care options offered by the church.

Activities. Spend most of this session on a tour of the nursery and preschool classes. Be sure to check with the teachers to let them know visitors will be coming. Ask the parents to look around the nursery and observe the interaction between the infants and the child care providers. When they observe the preschool classes, ask them to watch for moments of teaching the faith, both formal and informal.

Prior to the tour, show participants copies of the preschool curriculum. If there are forms to be filled out by parents of infants, hand out copies of that form. Allow ten minutes at the end of the session for a discussion of what the participants observed and any questions they may have.

Session Four: "Planning for the Baptism Day"

Purpose. The purpose of this session is to go over the congregation's baptismal liturgy.

Activities. Have copies of the liturgy available for everyone. Discuss the different parts of the liturgy and why they are included. Discuss any questions that are asked and make sure participants have time to ask about their role in the liturgy.

2. Booklets for Parents

The "It Takes a Village" story mentioned two booklets that a congregation can make available to parents. Development of these two booklets could be the joint responsibility of two congregational committees: Christian Education and Worship.

Booklet One: "The Church's Welcome—The Sacrament of Baptism"

Purpose. This booklet could be made available to adults awaiting the birth or adoption of a child or to new parents shortly after their child has come home. The booklet should explain the meaning and traditions of infant baptism as it is celebrated in the Christian tradition and in your congregation.

Cover and Format. The booklet can be simply designed and produced. Its complexity depends on the resources and money available for the project. A simple booklet stapled in the middle or held together with ribbon is sufficient. Consider using baptismal symbols on the cover. If there is an artist in your congregation (child, youth, or adult), ask her or him to work on a design for the cover.

Sections. You should include the following information in this booklet:

- *Introduction:* the purpose of the booklet
- *Christian baptism:* the biblical and theological meanings of baptism
- *The sacrament in this congregation:* how baptism takes place in worship in your congregation
- *Preparing for a child's baptism:* practical information about planning for baptism day, including the questions that are asked of parents at the baptism
- *Books and resources:* a listing of books and resources on the topic of baptism, available in the church library or office

Booklet Two: "Come unto Me—Children in the Life of This Congregation"

Purpose. This booklet can serve as an introduction to the variety of ways that children are included in the life, work, worship, and mission of your congregation. If your church has packets prepared to give to visitors or new members, this booklet should be included in that packet.

Such a booklet enables a congregation to specifically illustrate its commitment to nurturing children in the life of the Christian faith. It should be made available in pew racks or anywhere information about the church is publicly displayed.

Cover and Format. Invite a child to draw the cover for this booklet. If your church has access to color printing, the cover could be reproduced that way. If not, children could be asked to color the covers with crayons or markers. Make sure when you design the booklet that you have children and youth on the committee; the booklet should be aimed at children as well as adults. Think about symbols that could be used to identify each of the sections of the booklet.

Sections. You should include the following:

* *Introduction:* a statement about why children are important in the life of your congregation, possibly including a story about a child in the congregation
* *Children in worship:* the ways children participate in and lead worship services
* *Church school for children:* information on the church school setup and curriculum
* *Children as stewards:* the ways that children are included as stewards, sharing their time, talents, and money with the church
* *Children in service and mission:* how children can become involved in service and mission projects
* *Special opportunities for children:* a listing of the special opportunities available for children, such as children's choirs, after-school programs, and vacation church school
* *Learning and celebrating with others:* information on any intergenerational church events, including seasonal events such as Advent workshops, Holy Week meals, or Pentecost celebrations
* *Children's library:* a listing of children's books and videos available through the church

3. "More Than Water: Thinking Intentionally about the Nurturing and Liturgical Dimensions of Baptism": A Workshop for the Christian Education and Worship Committees

Since plans for a baptism are often the responsibility of the pastor, committees are rarely involved in discussions about this sacrament, either in terms of its meaning or its place in the liturgy. This one-session workshop is designed to enable those responsible for nurture and worship to have such a discussion.

Purpose. The purpose of the workshop is to help participants think about the meaning and practice of baptism, specifically the inclusion of children and youth, the liturgy, and congregational traditions.

Objectives. By the end of the session, participants will have had the chance to do the following:

- Discuss the meanings present in the sacrament of baptism and in the different parts of the liturgy.
- Identify and discuss traditions of the baptismal liturgy (both denominational and congregational).
- Name ways that the congregation is involved in beginning the nurturing process for a child at baptism.

Activities. From these suggested activities, choose those that are most appropriate for your setting:

- Have bulletins available from a baptism Sunday. Go over the different parts of the liturgy, explaining their meaning and place.
- Discuss the biblical background for baptism and its theological meanings.
- Discuss the questions asked of parents, sponsors, and the congregation during a baptism service. Discuss how the congregation can be helped to nurture children in the Christian faith.
- Consider ways that children and youth are involved in the sacrament of baptism. Is any thought given to their participation or leadership? How can they be included?
- Affirm the role of these committees in helping parents become aware of the intentionality of parenting for faith expression.

4. "Singing Our Faith": An Examination of Baptismal Hymns

This topic can stand alone or be used as part of one of the other models just discussed.

Purpose. The purpose is to discuss the meaning of baptism through singing and a discussion of baptismal hymns.

Objectives. Participants should have the chance to do the following:

- Identify and discuss the basic theological meanings of the sacrament of baptism.
- Read through and sing baptismal hymns included in the hymnbook and in other sources.

Activities. You will need to have Bibles and hymnbooks available for all participants. You will also need a piano and someone who can play the hymns.

Your session should include the following activities.

1. *Opening the session* (15 minutes): Begin by singing a familiar baptismal hymn, one that is used at baptisms in your congregation. Have the words of the hymn printed separately from the music, and ask participants to identify the meanings of baptism present in the text of the hymn. Then spend some time discussing the theological meanings of the sacrament. Use information from this chapter's "Beliefs and Meanings" section as a background for this part of the session. Have Bibles available, and ask people to recall the biblical background for the sacrament.

2. *Developing the session* (40 minutes): Invite participants to turn to the baptism section of their hymnbook and select hymns to sing and discuss. Having the texts of the hymns printed ahead of time makes discussion about their theological meanings easier. Notice which hymns have a particular focus on the baptism of children.

You can use *The New Century Hymnal* (United Church of Christ), *The Chalice Hymnal* (Disciples of Christ), and *The Presbyterian Hymnal* (Presbyterian Church [U.S.A.]) to help in your planning. The following hymns represent the work of contemporary hymn writers; if they are not included in your denomination's hymnbook, get copies of the words and music to use in this session.

"Wash, O God, Your Sons and Daughters" (words by Ruth Duck)
"Take Me to the Water" (African American spiritual)
"In Water We Grow" (words by Brian Wren)
"Wonder of Wonders, Here Revealed" (words by Jane Parker Huber)
"Out of Deep, Unordered Water" (words by Weisse Flaggen)

"Passed through the Waters" (words by Richard K. Avery and
Donald S. Marsh)
"Baptized in Water" (words by Michael A. Saward)
"With Grateful Hearts Our Faith Professing" (words by Fred
Kaan)
"Child of Blessing, Child of Promise" (words by Ronald S. Cole-
Turner)
"We Know That Christ Is Raised" (words by John Brownlow
Geyer)

3. *Concluding the session* (5 minutes): Summarize the themes that
have emerged from the hymns, and then end with the prayer used at
the conclusion of a baptism service in your church.

In Water We Grow

The following verse from a Brian Wren hymn names both the context
and the process of baptism:

In water we grow,
secure in the womb,
and speechlessly know
love's safety and room.
Baptizing and blessing
we publish for good
the freeing, caressing
safe keeping of God.[23]

Source: "In Water We Grow." Words: Brian Wren. Copyright © 1993 by
Hope Publishing Co., Carol Stream, IL 60188. All rights reserved. Used by
permission.

In water a baby is formed and grows. Water breaks, signaling a movement from growth inside a woman's body to growth outside in a place
that is less calm and quiet, less warm, less dark, less tight and secure.
At just the right moment, a baby literally breaks into a new world and
most times is welcomed with arms that are gentle, hands that caress, a
body that is warm, and a blanket that is soft. The voices and touches
that have been heard or felt through layers of water are now experienced much more intensely. Once safely in the world, the responsibil-

ity for keeping this child extends beyond the family to the household of faith.

The phrase "In water we grow" is descriptive of the renewal of thinking and action regarding the sacrament of baptism that is being experienced by many congregations today. This renewal represents an investment by these churches in making more explicit and intentional the relationship between the beginning of life and the beginning of a life of faith. Searle says "that in their own way children in fact play an extremely active, even prophetic, role in the household of faith."[24]

If we take seriously this welcome with water, then we must be ready for the way children nurture the household of faith. Robert Coles speaks of children as pilgrims. He defines *pilgrim* as "someone who thinks ahead, who wonders what's coming—and I mean spiritually. We are on a journey through the years—a pilgrim is—and we are trying to find out what our destination is, what awaits us when the bus or the train pulls in."[25]

The sacrament of baptism publicly affirms the connection between a child, a family, and a household of faith. The use of water, the sign and seal of God's presence, is a visible reminder that in water we grow. Coles expresses this relationship in the following way:

> So it is we connect with one another, move in and out of one another's lives, teach and heal and affirm one another, across space and time— all of us wanderers, explorers, adventurers, stragglers and ramblers, sometimes tramps or vagabonds, even fugitives, but now and then pilgrims: as children, as parents, as old ones about to take that final step, to enter that territory whose character none of us here ever knows. Yet how young we are when we start wondering about it all, the nature of the journey and of the final destination.[26]

The sacrament of baptism marks an important day in the life of a child, the child's family, and the child's family of faith gathered in worship. Another journey of faith has begun, and all who are there, all who witness the welcome with water, are partners with this child as she or he grows in faith. The nature of the household of faith has been changed forever because a new one has been welcomed, and this child shall lead them.

3 Living in Response to Our Baptism

The story is told of three ministers who came together and realized they shared a common problem, pigeons on the roof and in the bell tower. The first minister said he had tried to get rid of the pigeons by spraying them with water. In so doing, he had caused leaks in the roof, and the pigeons enjoyed the bath but never left. The second minister said she had tried putting up plastic snakes with the hope that these would scare away the pigeons. She had found that the pigeons enjoyed sitting on them. The third minister announced she had solved the problem. The others were astounded and immediately wanted to know what solution she had found to their common problem. She said, "It's fairly simple; I went up to the roof, baptized and confirmed them, and I haven't seen them since!"

Is this how the members of your congregation respond to baptism? The previous chapters have outlined the theological, liturgical, and educational issues central to a discussion of the ways we respond to our baptisms through communal life, worship, work, and ministry. In this chapter I will further explore this issue by discussing six tensions that exist in our theology and ministry. As you will see, the actions of the families and congregations participating in a baptism clearly indicate their understanding of the call to live in response to this sacrament.

Inherited Faith or Faith Formation?

A child is baptized within a liturgy that includes making a promise. The promise to nurture a child in the Christian faith is publicly affirmed by parents and by the household of faith gathered in public worship. Janet Fishburn reminds us that "Christian faith is not inherited; each generation, each individual must learn faith anew."[1] Though a family may have inherited the family and ecclesial tradition of infant baptism, it is essential that parents consider the commitment involved in faith formation.

Such commitment, Fishburn believes, is the servant ministry of parenthood. "For Christians, parenthood is both an act of faith and a servant ministry."[2] In choosing to give birth to or adopt a child and then present this child for baptism, parents are making explicit that such ministry is a priority in their life. The decision to make an investment in the Christian formation of a child is as important a decision as the decision to give birth or adopt.

The congregation, or household of faith, becomes a partner in this commitment. "Membership in a Christian community offers [parents] companionship in work that will test their faithfulness, patience, and perseverance. Regular worship, Bible study, and prayer are aids to faith, especially as these disciplines remind Christian parents of the presence of God's grace in all of life."[3]

When congregations and parents understand and accept their roles, a partnership is formed that enables the household of faith to work with parents in the Christian formation of their child. No one has to face this responsibility alone.

Momentary Interruption or Lifetime Commitment?

Birthday celebrations in families are usually wonderful occasions of party planning, gift giving, storytelling, and picture taking. We mark our growth with great festivity!

Baptism anniversaries, however, are rarely noted or celebrated in families. Assignments to confirmands to find out stories about their baptism send families scurrying to dig out long-lost information and memories.

In moments of daydreaming, I engage in a never-boring activity, thinking about what I want to do during retirement. I image myself being a part of a congregation, and I think about the ways my time and talents could be put to use. I would like to volunteer to work with a small group of people interested in designing and producing a baptism book to give to every family who brings their child for baptism. It would have places for photographs, comments about the day, and a list of family and friends who were there. It would include room for a copy of the order of worship and a special place for a baptismal card and certificate.

With everything that parents have to do to get a child dressed and ready for church, making such a journal is, of course, a low priority. Perhaps a congregation's help in recalling the meaning and the memory of their child's baptism would ensure that the sacrament becomes a life-forming occasion, not a momentary interruption.

Revolving Door or Welcome Mat?

Years of working as a church educator have given me the chance to observe the revolving door of confirmation. This reality is shared by churches across denominational lines.

Some families have just two ecclesial requirements for their children: infant baptism and adolescent participation in a confirmation program leading to church membership. The second is much more difficult to achieve than the first; teenagers can voice their opinion, which is often rebellious. Confirmation education can become a meaningless ritual to salve parental conscience if the time between baptism and confirmation has been devoid of Christian discipleship at home and within the household of faith.

Confirmation becomes a last-ditch effort for some parents. Somehow they believe their faith-forming responsibilities are over if only they can get their teenager to a confirmation class so she or he can make a public profession of faith. Their work is done, these parents believe; it's now up to the teenager to decide what priority the church has in her or his life. Thus this important decision is often left to a thirteen year old. And if the model the teenager sees is one of nominal church attendance with no habits of daily discipleship, what incentive is there for this young person to continue growing in the faith?

Equally problematic is the church that closes its eyes to the ways children and youth can be involved as active participants and leaders in the life of the congregation. Children can serve as liturgists in worship, greet worshipers, offer prayers. They can be involved in mission projects in the church and the community. They can understand concepts of stewardship; they can save their money and contribute to projects sponsored by the church.

The only answer to the problem of the revolving door is to ensure that the congregation takes seriously its baptismal vows by being a welcome mat to children and youth, allowing their full participation in service, worship, work, and learning. Having been welcomed with water, a child who is invited to really participate in a congregation's life and worship is much more likely to be willingly confirmed into a continuing yet transforming relationship with the household of faith.

Ministry To or Ministry With?

Many congregations pride themselves on the Christian education programs they offer to children and youth. Take a look a most church newsletters and worship bulletins. Notice the opportunities for faith formation specially designed for children and youth. These programs offer unique opportunities for children and youth to be together for Christian education and activities.

Such ministries include midweek programs, choirs, vacation church school, work-camp trips, confirmation classes, retreats, and weekday preschool sessions. These kinds of programs are attractive to families seeking a church home, and they are essential parts of a congregation's commitment to the Christian nurture it promises to offer at baptism.

However, such programs of ministry *for* children and youth need to be combined with an educational and theological understanding of ministry *to* children and youth. Just how well a congregation understands this concept is evident through observation.

Are there occasions when the household of faith is engaged in education and ministry across the ages? Are there opportunities for intergenerational learning in church school? Vacation church school planned in the early evenings over a week or a month offers opportunities for children and youth to meet and learn with one another.

Are mission and ministry in the community limited to adults working with adults? My sister's church once organized a group of children and adults to work at a community food pantry packing food boxes for homeless persons. When she arrived at the pantry, she immediately knew that the director of the pantry was disappointed upon seeing the children. The director had assumed that more adults would be coming from the church and thus that more food boxes could be packed. The children and youth began to work, talking about what they were doing and its purpose.

By the end of their time at the pantry, the director admitted she was pleasantly surprised at the amount of work the group had done. My nephew talked for several days about his work at the food pantry. I occasionally ask him about this experience, and I hear his questions and listen to him reflect on what he saw, heard, and accomplished. In so doing, he ministers to me.

Congregations in general and adults in particular miss opportunities to be in ministry *with* children and youth when they are content to allow a few people (often parents) to be responsible for age-appropriate ministry *to* children and youth. If the church is to have a future, it is essential that adults claim the promise of their baptismal vows. The church will die if adults past the age of child bearing and rearing continue to say, "I did that once, it's someone else's turn." The promise made at a child's baptism is one we must strive to fulfill as long as that child is alive; the waters of baptism remind us of our calling to be in ministry.

Social Ritual or Abundant Water?

I sometimes imagine that I am an architect, and I think about how I would design a building for a congregation that took seriously their commitment to sacramental education. I would first want to rethink the baptismal font or bowl. I have been in some churches where there is no visible symbol of the sacraments. The communion table is placed far away from the people as an altar, and it is used only to hold flowers on most Sundays. I have watched a bowl magically appear for a baptism and then disappear into a closet awaiting the next call. I have seen wooden fonts with tops, ornate metal fonts, and intricately designed ceramic fonts. Except in large sanctuaries, baptismal fonts are usually very small, just large enough to dip your hand in and scoop out a bit of water.

I would design a font with two pieces: a bottom stand made of pottery or wood by some artist in the congregation, and on top of the stand, a bowl made of glass so the water would be visible to everyone. This font would always be standing at the back of the sanctuary filled with water. On Sundays when there was a baptism, it would be moved to the front.

The abundant water in the font would be a visible reminder of the meaning of the sacrament, that to which we are called every day. The font would be placed in the back so that people would have to walk around it to enter the sanctuary. It would thus interrupt their path, perhaps causing them to stop, place their hands in the water, and remember their promise, the ethical implications of a lifetime of faithful Christian living. Each time we take an intentional step to remember, recall, and recommit, we ensure that baptism will not become an empty social ritual in the life of our households of faith.

Liturgical and Daily Rhythms

I once flew home with two small nephews accompanying me. They were so excited about flying to Chicago that they could not sit still waiting for the plane to arrive, then to take off, then to land. Riding in a taxi, I gave thanks for an understanding cab driver who patiently answered each question from the curious five- and seven-year-old boys.

After a quick trip to the grocery store to pick out favorite breakfast cereals, gelatin to make jigglers, and other necessities, we settled in to our time together. Lincoln Logs came out and backpacks were unzipped to reveal dinosaurs, a worn brown bear, and a rather tattered quilt. Playing together for these two is not always easy. Toys had to be negotiated, space had to be shared.

I quickly prepared a light summer meal and called them to the dinner table. We decided which of the favorite blessings would be sung, and I watched with tears in my eyes as these two boys got on their knees in their chairs so they could reach across the table to hold each other's hand. We sang, with great gusto, "God is Great" and the Johnny Appleseed blessing.

I was touched by their connection to each other, which sometimes provokes conflict but at this moment evoked family ties and thanksgiving to God. I felt blessed by their presence and the way they nurture my faith.

In the intensity, diversity, and rapid pace of our daily lives, we must remember to reconnect the holy and sacred with the daily and ordinary. How can the liturgy of the sacrament of baptism become the rhythm of our daily lives? What is the connection between this sacrament and a faithful Christian life? Living in response to our baptism is our vocation as Christians. This vocation extends to the congregation in its responsibility to nurture families.

Liturgical and Educational Models

The following learning opportunities offer practical methods to help your congregation learn to live in response to baptism. The first two models are simply outlined to get your thinking started. The model for an adult class is fully designed for use in an appropriate setting.

1. "Preparing to Come to Worship": A Workshop for Young Children

An important marker in the lives of young children is the transition from child care during worship to full participation in the service. Many churches seek to ease this transition by offering a session or sessions to help children learn about worship and their participation in the community of faith.

Here you will find an outline for a one-session introduction to worship for young children and their parents. Use it as a starting point for planning your own workshop. It is important to build this workshop into the planning calendar of the church so it takes place in late August or early September to coincide with the transition of young children from one grade to another.

Purpose. The purpose of this program is to teach young children about the different parts of a worship service and help them learn the ways they can participate and lead in worship.

Objectives. By the end of this workshop, learners will have had the chance to do the following:

• Identify the different parts of the worship service.
• Practice saying or singing the responses used in the liturgy.
• Talk about the ways they can be involved in worship.

Activities. From this list of activities, select those that work best for your workshop:

1. Visit the sanctuary and talk about the different parts of the room and their function: the pulpit, communion table, baptismal font, lectern, paraments, and so forth.
2. Invite your minister to meet with the children for a brief time to talk about her or his role in worship. Ask the minister to wear the robe (and stole) she or he normally wears and to be prepared to talk about why it is worn.
3. Have bulletins available. If your church prints children's bulletins, use these to go over the different parts of the worship service. Most liturgies follow this basic order:

• The people gather (call to worship, hymn, confession, and assurance)
• The word (read and proclaimed)
• Response to the word (affirmation of faith, prayers of the people, offering)
• The people go out (hymn, benediction)

4. Invite the children to role-play some of the different parts of the service.
5. Brainstorm ways that the children could lead in worship. (They could serve as greeters, take up the offering, read the scripture, bring flowers, help prepare for communion, draw a bulletin cover, sing in a children's choir, and so forth.)
6. Teach the responses (spoken and sung) used in worship on a regular basis.
7. Have paper and markers available for children to draw pictures of the sanctuary.
8. Talk with the children about the purpose of congregational worship. "We come together to worship God because . . ."
9. Sing some of the hymns or songs that will be used in worship during the next month.

10. Some congregations have worship bags available for young children to pick up as they enter the sanctuary. These bags are made of cloth and contain, for example, a children's worship bulletin, colored markers or crayons, a clipboard for use in writing or coloring, and a children's Bible storybook. If your church has such bags available, show them to the children and explain their purpose.

Resources. The following resources may be useful in your planning for this workshop:

• Carolyn Carter Brown, *Forbid Them Not, Involving Children in Sunday Worship,* years A, B, and C (Nashville: Abingdon Press, 1994).
• Mary Duckert, *New Kid in the Pew, Shared Ministry with Children* (Louisville: Westminster/John Knox, 1991).
• David Ng and Virginia Thomas, *Children in the Worshiping Community* (Louisville: John Knox Press, 1981). See Chapter 6, "Teaching about Worship in Graded Groups."
• Elizabeth J. Sandell, *Including Children in Worship, A Planning Guide for Congregations* (Minneapolis: Augsburg Fortress, 1991).
• "Children as Participants in Corporate Worship," in *Reformed Liturgy and Music* 26, no. 1 (winter 1992). Also see the articles by David Ng, "Encouraging Children to Hear the Word of God," and Cynthia Weeks Logan, "Helping Children Learn to Worship."
• Gail Ramshaw, *Sunday Morning* (Chicago: Liturgy Training Publications, 1993).

2. "Worship with All God's People": An Intergenerational Class

Even though we participate in worship on a weekly basis, rarely do we take the time to think about the liturgy and what it means to worship together as a congregation. The four sessions of this class (each one hour in length) could be offered during the summer or spread out during the year in different liturgical seasons. The activities suggested for the previous model are also appropriate for this class.

Session One: "We Worship"

Purpose. The purpose of this session is to discuss the reason we come together in worship: we worship in grateful response to God our Creator, Redeemer, and Sustainer.

Session Two: "Worship in Our Congregation"

Purpose. The purpose of this session is to become familiar with the different parts of the worship service and discuss the reasons they are part of the liturgy.

Session Three: "Hearing God's Word"

Purpose. The purpose of this session is to experience different ways that God's story can be communicated.

Session Four: "Seasons of the Church Year"

Purpose. The purpose of this session is to become familiar with the different seasons of the church year and their meaning for us in worship.

Activities. Consider the following activities for your class:

1. Set up learning centers that teach about the seasons of the church year: Advent, Christmas, Epiphany and the season of Epiphany, Ash Wednesday, Lent, Holy Week, Easter, and Pentecost. Plan activities to help participants learn about the colors, symbols, stories, and songs particular to each of the seasons.
2. Help learners become familiar with the scripture lessons that will be read during a one-month period. Learners could read the lessons, illustrate them, sing hymns related to them, or act them out.
3. Make banners to use during the different seasons of the church year.

3. "Parenting for Faith Expression": A Workshop on Living Faithfully with Children

Living faithfully with children and youth means we are comfortable with the faith we affirm in our own lives. It also means we feel at home with the questions, wonderings, and honesty of children. Often, adults feel that teaching children about faith is a matter of formal learning. On the contrary, children and youth learn as much or more about faith by watching how we live and what we say.

The "Parenting for Faith Expression" model that follows is for an adult class of four one-hour sessions.[4] It could be offered during church school on four Sundays or once a week in the evening for a month. The primary audience for this class is parents, adult relatives, and anyone else interested in nurturing the spiritual life of young people.

Resources. You will need the following resources to teach this class:

- Robert Coles, *The Spiritual Life of Children* (Boston: Houghton Mifflin, 1990).
- David Heller, *Talking to Your Child about God: A Book for Families of All Faiths* (New York: Bantam, 1988).
- Harold S. Kushner, *When Children Ask about God: A Guide for Parents Who Don't Always Have All the Answers* (New York: Schocken Books, 1989).
- Gretchen Wolff Pritchard, *Offering the Gospel to Children* (Boston: Cowley Publications, 1992).
- John Westerhoff, *Bringing Up Children in the Christian Faith* (Minneapolis: Winston Press, 1980).

Session One: "Listening to Children"

Purpose. The purpose of this session is to introduce the class and explore the topic of how we listen to children when they speak about God.

Objectives. By the end of this session, learners will have had the opportunity to do the following:

- Meet each other and become familiar with the names and ages of the children represented by the families in the class.
- Get an overview of the focus of the four sessions and identify any additional concerns that should be addressed.
- Hear children's stories from Robert Coles's book *The Spiritual Life of Children.*

Room Setup. Set up the room with chairs in a circle or people seated at tables, whichever arrangement suits the number of people you are expecting. Have pictures and posters of children placed around the room. (Argus is a good source for such posters; they can be found in bookstores or school supply stores.) Make sure to have pictures of children representing the multiethnic reality of our world today.

It would also be a good idea to have a resource table set up for the four sessions. For the first two weeks, display books for children. Then display books for adults during the final two weeks of the workshop.

Activities. This session should include the following activities:

1. *Introducing the session* (15 minutes): Begin the class with prayer and a story from Coles's book, and then introduce the topic of the class. Give people time to introduce themselves, the children in their lives, and an issue that is particularly important to them. If the group is smaller than ten, stay together for the introductions. If the group is larger, ask people to meet each other in triads. Then ask the triads to introduce themselves and share their concerns for this class.

2. *Developing the session* (40 minutes): Prepare a twenty- to thirty-minute presentation on children's comments about God based on your reading of Coles's book. I have found the following parts of the book especially helpful in teaching this part of the session: from Chapter 4, "The Voice of God," the stories of Haroon, Avram, Anne, and Margarita; from Chapter 5, "Young Spirituality," the discussion about the power of biblical stories; and from Chapter 13, the concept of the child as pilgrim.

Use the remaining time for a discussion of these questions: What have you heard your or another child say or ask about God recently? What did you learn from his or her statement or question? What response did you make?

3. *Concluding the session* (5 minutes): Give a brief overview of the next session. Ask people to bring Bibles with them to the next session and to respond to the questions on page 44.

Conclude the session by recalling the children's statements offered by the participants and then using these statements in a closing litany. Ask those who will to share a child's statement, and after each one the group should respond, "Be present with me in the life of this child, O God." Ask everyone to be especially attentive to the comments of children and youth this week and to be prepared to share what they have heard.

A Faith to Live and Share

1. To say that I believe in God means . . .

2. Faith involves . . .

3. Who or in what times or places have you felt nurtured and supported in your own life of faith?

4. What makes you struggle with belief and faith?

5. What commitments do you make in your life to your own spiritual growth—prayer, reading the Bible, study with other adults, participation in worship?

Session Two: "A Faith to Share"

Purpose. The purpose of this session is to reflect on the faith we affirm and live, the faith we must share with children and youth.

Objectives. By the end of this session, learners will have had the opportunity to do the following:

• Identify the places and times when we are nurtured and supported in our faith.
• Discuss what makes us struggle with belief and faith.
• Define and discuss what we mean by belief and faith.

Room Setup. Set up the room so that people are seated at tables. In the middle of the tables have Bibles available as well as pictures and articles from newspapers and news magazines. These pictures and articles should represent some of the forces that help and hinder our attempts to live the Christian faith in today's world.

Activities. There are several videos available for rent or purchase from Ecufilm (1-800-251-4091) that could be used in this session. For example, "Discovering Everyday Spirituality" with host Thomas Moore includes six programs on three videotapes. Each program is twenty-five minutes long and comes with a study guide. (The workshop can be expanded to one or more additional sessions if videos are used.)

The video series "Questions of Faith" highlights a dozen contemporary thinkers reflecting on their life of faith. Each video is twenty to thirty minutes long and comes with a study guide. If you use this video series, appropriate topics for discussion include Who Is God? What Good Is Prayer? What's God Got to Do with Evil? What Matters, Anyway?

The following design for this session assumes that you are not using a video:

1. *Introducing the session* (15 minutes): Begin the session by reading a psalm and an opening prayer. Ask people to look at the clippings on the table and then relate them to our attempts to live a life of faith. How would they explain these pictures or articles to young children?

2. *Developing the session* (40 minutes): This part of the session can be developed in several ways. One way is to explore definitions of faith and belief. Begin with the questions that participants were to bring to class. Start with questions 1 and 2, asking for volunteers to

share their responses. If people seem interested in continuing this discussion, use some of the quotations that follow to discuss what others have said about faith and belief.

The word *credo* means literally "I believe." According to Sara Little, who translates the word as "I set my heart," credos or beliefs are "avenues by which we interpret and thereby reappropriate at deeper levels the meaning of the Christian faith—meaning which becomes reality and not formulations about reality." She continues, "Belief emerges out of and in turn informs faith."[5]

According to C. Ellis Nelson, "Faith is communicated by a community of believers . . . the meaning of faith is developed by its members out of their history, by their interaction with each other, and in relationship to the events that take place in their lives."[6]

Christian belief systems have four functions, says Little: "to help a person make sense of the world and have a frame of reference for understanding, caring, deciding and doing; to aid a community, the church, to achieve identity and maintain community; to link human experience and the Christian tradition through an interpretation that internalizes meaning and gives direction to life; to link lives of individuals and communities to larger, ultimate realities and purposes."[7]

According to the Presbyterian Church, "Faith includes particular beliefs about God, the world, and ourselves. . . . Faith gives rise to a new kind of life. The 'life of faith' is the way of living that is organized by and flows out of faith. In the life of faith, we become more and more to participate in the new reality God is opening to us. . . . Above all, the life of faith involves rejoicing in the love and grace of God, giving thanks to God secure in the knowledge that all God's promises are sure, and sharing that love and grace in the life of the world."[8]

After this discussion of the meaning of beliefs, participants can share their answers to questions 3, 4, and 5 on the handout. If the sharing is done in small groups, give time for reporting back to the entire group. Be prepared to share your own responses to these questions.

3. *Concluding the session* (5 minutes): Remind participants that the topic for the next session is "Dealing with Difficult Questions." Ask them to suggest issues they would like to address during this session. Have index cards available for those who would like to write down their concerns.

Session Three: "Dealing with Difficult Questions"

Purpose. The purpose of this session is to address specific issues of concern to the participants. Possible topics include death, illness, and divorce.

Objectives. By the end of this session, learners will have had the opportunity to do the following:

- Identify issues of concern to class members.
- Discuss the issues and how they relate to the lives and faith of children and their families.
- Become familiar with resources for parents.

Activities. This session should include the following activities.

1. *Introducing the session* (15 minutes): Begin the session by reading a children's book to the group. (Appropriate books are listed at the end of this model.)

2. *Developing the session* (40 minutes): The content of this session will depend on the issues the group want to discuss. Some of the resource books listed here can be of great help with certain topics. For instance, in his book *Talking to Your Child about God,* David Heller does an excellent job of addressing the problems faced by interfaith families. In the chapter "Discussing God's Role in the World," he also confronts the difficult issues of suffering and war.

Harold Kushner's book *When Children Ask about God: A Guide for Parents Who Don't Always Have All the Answers* has some excellent discussions, including those in the chapters "Children Ask about God" and "Don't Blame God for 'Acts of God.'" In the latter, he discusses suffering and evil, death, reward and punishment, and bad people.

Sometimes adults need help in ministry with children who are experiencing a particular crisis in their life, such as divorce, grief, abuse, hospitalization, terminal illness, or disability. Andrew Lester's book *When Children Suffer* (Louisville: Westminster Press, 1987) is an excellent resource. It provides helpful information on comforting a child and her or his parents, as well as a discussion of faith issues related to particular concerns.

3. *Concluding the session* (5–10 minutes): End the session by mentioning books that parents will find particularly helpful in dealing

with difficult issues with their children. Close with a quote about life-times from the book *Lifetimes*, by Bryan Mellonie and Robert Ingpen.

Remind parents that the important thing in helping their children through difficult times or questions is not that they (the parents) have to have all the answers. What is most essential is that children know they are loved by their parent/s.

Session Four: "Resources for Faith Sharing"

Purpose. The purpose of this session is to become familiar with resources available for parents and other adults who spend time with children.

Objectives. By the end of this session, learners will have had the opportunity to do the following:

• Become familiar with resources for use in family faith sharing.
• Identify personal commitments to faith sharing.

Room Setup. Set up several learning centers in the room. At each learning center, have books available on tables for participants examine. Topics for the centers could include books for reading with younger children; resources for parents; resources for nurturing your life of faith; and bible storybooks for use with children.

Activities. This session should include the following activities.

1. *Introducing the session* (10 minutes): Begin with a reading of Deut. 6: 4–9 and an opening prayer. Read another children's book to the group, such as *In God's Name* by Sandy Eisenberg Sasso.

2. *Developing the session* (45 minutes): Explain to the group that they will have thirty minutes to look over the resources displayed on the tables. Then they will come together for a final presentation and discussion. Base this presentation on your reading of books by Kushman, Gellman and Hartman, and Westerhoff.

Remind participants that the spiritual life we share with children is really a very simple thing. As Kushman states, when we make statements about God with children, we are really trying to "recognize when God comes into our lives."[9] In their book *Where Does God Live?* Gellman and Hartman suggest five guidelines for conversations with children about God: "Let your child watch you do the religious things you do. . . . Tell your children what you believe, while making it clear to them that they must decide for themselves what they believe. . . . Don't be afraid to say 'I don't know' when talking to your child about God. . . . Try to relate God to how we live, not just to what we believe. . . . Don't give answers about God which are too simple."[10]

In his book *Bringing Up Children in the Christian Faith,* John Westerhoff lists his own five guidelines for sharing faith with children: "We need to tell and retell the biblical story—the stories of faith—together. We need to celebrate our faith and our lives. We need to pray together. We need to listen and talk to each other. We need to perform faithful acts of service and witness together."[11]

3. *Concluding the session* (5 minutes): Pass out paper and envelopes and ask the participants to write a letter to themselves. Ask them to put in the letter things they would like to remember from this class, commitments they would like to make, ideas they would like to try. When everyone is finished, ask them to put their letter in an envelope and address it to themselves. Tell them you will mail these letters in three months.

Conclude the session with prayer.

Resources. You should include the following books in your learning centers:

Books for Reading with Younger Children
- Jane Cowen-Fletcher, *It Takes a Village* (New York: Scholastic, 1994).
- Sharon Greenlee, *When Someone Dies* (Atlanta: Peachtree Publishers, 1992).
- Bijou Le Tord, *The River and the Rain: The Lord's Prayer* (New York: Doubleday, 1994).
- Bryan Mellonie and Robert Ingpen, *Lifetimes: The Beautiful Way to Explain Death to Children* (New York: Bantam, 1983).
- Doris Sanford, *It Must Hurt a Lot: A Child's Book about Death* (Portland, Oreg.: Multnomah Press, 1986). This is one in a series of books and videos for children ages five to eleven made available by A Corner of the Heart, located in Milwaukie, Oregon. Other books in the series focus on divorce and sexual abuse.
- Sandy Eisenberg Sasso, *In God's Name* (Woodstock, Vt.: Jewish Lights Publishing, 1994). This is a wonderful book for children

and adults that illustrates the varieties of ways we come to know
God. Sasso has also written *God's Paintbrush,* which invites
children to meet God in the common events of their lives.

Resources for Parents
- Jean Grasso Fitzpatrick, *Something More: Nurturing Your
  Child's Spiritual Growth* (New York: Viking, 1991).
- Marc Gellman and Thomas Hartman, *How Do You Spell God?
  Answers to the Big Questions from around the World* (New York:
  Morrow Junior Books, 1995).
- Maria Harris, *The Faith of Parents* (Mahwah, N.J.: Paulist Press,
  1991).
- David Heller, *Talking to Your Child about God: A Book for Fam-
  ilies of All Faiths* (New York: Bantam, 1988). Also see his *The
  Children's God* (Chicago: University of Chicago Press, 1986).
- Ina Hughes, *A Prayer for Children* (New York: William Morrow
  and Company, 1995).
- Harold S. Kushner, *When Children Ask about God: A Guide for
  Parents Who Don't Always Have All the Answers* (New York:
  Schocken Books, 1989).
- Kathleen McGinnis and Barbara Oehlberg, *Starting Out Right:
  Nurturing Young Children as Peacemakers* (Oak Park, Ill.:
  Meyer Stone Books, 1988).
- Gretchen Wolff Pritchard, *Offering the Gospel to Children*
  (Boston: Cowley Publications, 1992).
- Betsy Dawn Inskeep Smylie and John Sherian Smylie, *Christian
  Parenting* (Nashville: Upper Room, 1991).

Resources for Nurturing Your Life of Faith
- Polly Berrien Berends, *Gently Lead: How to Teach Your Children
  about God While Finding Out for Yourself* (New York: Harper-
  Perennial, 1991).
- Robert Coles, *The Spiritual Life of Children* (Boston: Houghton
  Mifflin, 1990).
- John Westerhoff, *Bringing Up Children in the Christian Faith*
  (New York: Harper, 1980). Also see his *Will Our Children Have
  Faith?* (New York: Seabury Press, 1973).

Bible Storybooks for Use with Children
• Marc Gellman, *God's Mailbox* (New York: Morrow Junior Books, 1996).
• Marc Gellman and Oscar de Mejo, *Does God Have a Big Toe? Stories about Stories in the Bible* (New York: Harper and Row, 1989).
• Andrew Knowles, *The Crossroad Children's Bible* (New York: Crossroad Publishing, 1983).

Immersed in Living

The last verse of a Brian Wren hymn on the baptism of Jesus asks for God's help:

Faith rests content with questions
Of when and why and how,
But craves the gift of seeing
What God is doing now.
Christ, bring us to our Jordan
Of newly opened eyes,
Through love, immersed in living,
As you were once baptized.[12]

Source: "Christ, When You Came to Jordan." Words: Brian Wren. Copyright © 1983 by Hope Publishing Co., Carol Stream, IL 60188. All rights reserved. Used by permission.

Listening to a child requires that you enter her or his world. I am reminded of this fact each time I have a conversation with my nephew. I realize that he is telling me something that he has been thinking about, and sometimes he starts in midstream, so to speak—he involves me at the midpoint of his thinking, and I have to get him to back up.

For example, he started talking about beehives and how they cost twenty dollars. I thought to myself, oh, Josh has been reading about bees and decided it might be a good idea to get a hive and watch bees make honey. My next thought was, have his parents lost their mind? I kept listening. He continued to talk about bees and how they had only raised enough money for two hives but somebody gave them twenty dollars and they were able to get three hives. "Isn't that neat?" he said. "Yes, that's neat," I replied, not really sure what I was affirming.

So I asked him to tell me about the bees. That's when I learned that his church school class had been collecting money to buy bees through the Heifer Project, which sends animals to people and countries that need them. Josh told me that the bees were given to people so they could the get the honey and use it for food or sell it to make money to buy food.

Children are very "immersed in living." They are intensely involved in living each day, in playing, in asking questions, making connections, trying to make sense of the world they inhabit. "Why do people litter? Don't they know that it's not good for the earth?" "Why did those people shoot out our gas lights? That's called vandalism. Why do people do that?" "Why do people hurt children?"

The honesty of their questions, their fears and their affirmations remind us of their deep immersion in the daily activity of living on this earth. How attuned are we to their presence among us?

Leontine Kelly reminds us that baptism "is choosing the gift of God and renewing with each day's breath the blessed intention to be God's forever!"[13] Two recent volumes of the journal *Reformed Liturgy and Music* have focused on the sacrament of baptism. In reading the second volume in this series, I was struck by the implications of two parts of the liturgy of baptism: the significance of the vows of renunciation, and the act itself of bringing a child for baptism.

I must admit that the questions focusing on the renunciation of evil have never made sense to me until recently.[14] I have had a difficult time sensing the presence of evil when holding an infant in my arms. I now understand that the reality of evil in our world must not only be confronted, but named and challenged. According to J. Frederick Holper, "The church has discovered that confrontation with evil is at the heart of the gospel, and therefore needs to be at the heart of the sacrament of Christian identity and vocation, namely, baptism."[15]

The renunciation of evil asks that parents "turn from the ways of sin and renounce evil and its power in the world."[16] Parents are then asked to profess their faith in Jesus Christ as Sovereign and Savior. This turning from sin and evil and turning to Christ and his grace and love is a visible affirmation of the reality of the faith we profess in a world in which we are a minority voice.

Unless we are involved in naming the evil in the world, keeping it in front of us so we know who we are and what we are being called to do, then we could slip into the silence of racism, sexism, and ageism. We could fail to see the poor, the homeless, and the suffering among us, the forces of evil at work to tear us apart, human from human and country from country.

At the moment when parents are asked to renounce evil during a baptismal liturgy, I would like to turn to the congregation and ask them to name the evils of the world that day. Such naming could remind them that through this sacrament, they stand with the parents and their child in working as a faith community for bringing into the world God's justice, righteousness, and peace.

Brett Webb-Mitchell is a consistent voice for children with disabilities within the community of faith. In writing (with Stanley Hauerwas) about the act of bringing children with mental retardation for baptism, he reminds us that in the act of baptism, "no longer is the child perceived as an individual, independent person, but is now understood as a child of the New Covenant, to be raised in the Christian faith not by the parents only, but by the congregation as a whole. . . . The child with a disability is one of the children of God, . . . who cares for the child through the act of the community of Christ as a whole."[17]

In a world that increasingly values individual achievement, it is comforting to remember that as Christians we are called to be immersed in living by first being immersed in faithful Christian communities, households of God that struggle to support and care for each other. Say Webb-Mitchell and Hauerwas: "[Baptism] is a common act, commonly done, that constitutes God's people for a world that worships not our God. Without this sacramental act, we literally could not be."[18]

With this sacramental act, we join with Christians throughout the ages in boldly walking with water on our foreheads to immerse ourselves in the living to which God calls us.

4 Setting the Table

Special occasions call for a celebration. Planning for the celebration begins the process. Sometimes invitations are mailed, or people are invited by a phone call or in person. As the time for the celebration draws near, preparations begin.

Questions and worries immediately come to mind. Who will be able to come? What food will we serve? Is there enough room for all who are invited? We want everyone to have a good time.

Preschool children get caught up in the enthusiasm of planning, especially if it is their own birthday party, and wonder if the day will ever arrive. Older and more experienced children know that with the guests come gifts, and so they wonder what they will receive from those invited.

The anticipated day arrives with much excitement. Everyone seems to enjoy themselves. Friends greet one another, conversations ensue, and food is shared. People leave the celebration feeling happy to have been included and warmly welcomed by this family or group of friends.

The meal we eat as a community of faith, as God's household, involves many of the same elements as a celebration at home. Planning and preparation, invitations, sharing of a meal, and leaving are essential parts of the liturgy of communion.

The meal is not a fancy one. The bread may be whole wheat, herb, pita, or white. It can be cut into squares, torn from a loaf, or eaten as wafers. The cup may contain wine or juice. The simplicity of this meal belies the intricacies of meanings and feelings inherent in the feast we call the Eucharist, Holy Communion, or the Lord's Supper.

In a culture where mealtimes at a table with family are more an exception than a rule, it becomes essential to reconsider the meaning and practice of the meal we prepare and eat in remembrance of Jesus Christ. This chapter focuses on the following questions, which address key issues related to the whole family of God eating at the table:

1. Are children truly welcome at Christ's Table? What enables their participation? What prohibits their participation?
2. What beliefs and meanings grow out of our experience of this sacrament? How do these beliefs and meanings help to nurture a life of Christian faith?
3. What is the role of the congregation and the family in preparing children to come to the table?
4. What educational and liturgical models enable the feeding and Christian nurture of children and youth who eat at the table?

The two stories that follow can help us frame some of the cognitive, theological, and liturgical issues addressed in this chapter.

The Table Is Set

The congregation was gathering for worship on the first day of the month, communion Sunday. Friends were greeting each other. Visitors were being welcomed. Children were looking for their parents. Youth were finding places to sit together. The reverent quietness of the room was quickly being replaced by holy noise, the noise of conversation and greetings, of hugs and handshakes.

The choir and the minister appeared, and as the organ began to play, the congregation began to prepare themselves to worship God. The communion table had been set. A white cloth covered the table, and the cup and the bread were brought down by two children and placed in the middle of the table. There was enough of this holy food for all to share.

The children were waiting for the special time they knew was theirs. It finally came—not soon enough for some active three year olds and their parents. The minister invited the children to come forward. It was heavenly chaos as children scrambled out of their seats into the aisles and came down the steps from the balcony, some holding on to a parent's hand, some very proudly on their own.

The minister shared a story about stewardship, gave each child a story paper to take home, and ended this special time with a prayer. Adults helped lead the younger children out of the sanctuary to the preschool rooms, while the older children returned to their seats to join their family and friends.

As one four-year-old boy went by the communion table on his way out of the sanctuary, he noticed the table and how it was set. It looked very pretty to him. The table was filled with trays of small cups of juice and a beautiful loaf of bread. He touched the bread lightly with his fingers as he went by and then looked up and said, "I want some of that bread." As he got closer to the door of the sanctuary, he said it again, making sure he had been heard and understood: "I want some of that bread."

His request was simple: "I want some of that bread." I remembered thinking that same thing when I was a child, but my request had always been silent, not spoken with such authority. Because communion was tied to confirmation (joining the church), I had sat in the pew with my family while the plate and the cup were passed over and around me. I had always wondered why I couldn't eat the bread and drink from the cup. Why was I excluded from something that obviously was powerful, almost mystical, and to a child's eyes, magical and unknown?

"I want some of that bread," he asked. At a Christmas Eve service two years before, he had walked down the aisle with his family to take communion, and he had been given some of that bread and was told, "God loves you, Josh." So I thought about his request for bread. I thought about his leaving the service before he would get that bread, and I wondered what to do, knowing he would not forget his request.

As I went forward to take communion, I decided what to do. After worship was over, I went to the table and took a piece of bread from the loaf and a cup from the tray and went to find Josh. There in the hall, we communed.

Places at the Table

A grandfather had been a lifelong member of the United Church of Christ. He was accustomed to and believed in the practice of inviting children to Christ's Table only after their confirmation. He had held this point of view for many years.

Then one day he went to visit his son and family in another community. There was no UCC church in that community, and the family was reluctantly attending a church of another denomination. As in the United Church of Christ, this church served only those children who had been confirmed. The family understood that their daughter would not be included in the sacrament. When it came time for communion, the family went forward to receive. Not wanting to be left alone in the pew, the girl went with her family, knowing she couldn't share in the meal.

As the minister begin distributing the elements, one of the things he said was, "This table is spread for all those who love the Savior Jesus Christ." When he reached the family, as expected he skipped over the girl.

And then in a voice loud enough to be heard all over the church, the girl said, "Why can't I have some? I love Jesus too." She had been listening carefully.

In that instant, in that split second, the grandfather's opinion on the subject made a 180-degree turn. His tightly held theology, his cherished traditions, his comfortable practices, "the way he'd always done it," all fell away. It just didn't work anymore. And this grandfather found himself asking, "Why can't she have some? She loves Jesus too!"[1]

As the grandfather came to realize, Christ's Table is not always an open one. Children and youth are not welcome at the table when

- *the old, old story we love to tell, the good news of Jesus Christ, is not lived out in the invitation we offer at the table, where Jesus is the host;*
- *a ticket for admission (confirmation) is required in order to share in the meal;*
- *participation is based on a supposed mastery of the correct amount and type of knowledge;*
- *they are asked to leave before the meal is served;*
- *they are not regular participants in worship and thus do not know the rituals, expectations, and norms of their worshiping community;*
- *the liturgy consistently uses language beyond their comprehension and experience;*

- *they are never included in the preparation or serving of the meal;*
- *they are not taught the parts of the liturgy appropriate to their level of understanding and participation;*
- *the practices, responses, and meanings of the sacrament are never openly discussed or explained to them either at home or at church;*
- *we don't take seriously the simplicity and complexity of their faith and their faith questions.*

Beliefs and Meanings

The last twenty years have seen significant changes in the ways that many mainline denominations have thought about Holy Communion and who is welcome at the table. Until the late 1970s, polity prevented children in some denominations from participating in the meal. As I have mentioned, their admission to the table was tied to confirmation, joining the church. Thankfully, today the United Church of Christ, the Presbyterian Church (U.S.A.), the United Methodist Church, and other denominations within the reformed family of faith have changed their polity to welcome baptized children to Christ's Table. These changes have enabled a more honest recognition and affirmation of the meaning of the sacrament of communion.

In writing about baptism, which he calls "the Lord's welcome," John Burkhart says that at the occasion of a baptism, "the assembly is never the same again, for the new have been added; and the assembly is not free to pick and choose among those who have been given the Lord's welcome and are clothed with Christ."[2] Burkhart concludes that "lest the host be offended at the way welcomed guests are treated, none of those so welcomed is to be kept from the feast."[3]

For Burkhart, the relationship between the sacraments of baptism and communion is easily seen and understood: The welcome we extend as a community of faith to the newest one baptized in our midst should be further extended to a seat at the table where we are guests and Jesus Christ is the host.

As Christians were beginning to rethink their attitudes toward communion, the Presbyterian Church prepared materials to help congregations implement new practices of welcoming children and youth to Christ's Table. In one such pamphlet, *A Theology of the Lord's Sup-*

per, Catherine Gunsalus Gonsalez has also noted the relationship between the two sacraments. "Baptism points to our participation in the death and resurrection of Jesus. So also does communion. . . . If baptism is the engrafting into Christ, the Lord's Supper is the continuous nourishment from the root that any graft needs if it is to stay alive. Jesus is the vine, and we are the branches [John 15:5]. Baptism is the sign and seal of the beginning of our new life in Christ. Communion is the seal of the feeding of that new life."[4]

Gonsalez suggests that the promises made at a baptism are remembered and fulfilled at communion. "Baptism calls us to repentance, and communion repeats that call. Baptism assures us that such repentance will be met with forgiveness, and communion visibly brings that assurance to us."[5]

The United Church of Christ's statement of faith makes clear this connection in a single sentence: "By baptism, a person becomes a member of Christ's church, and is welcomed at Christ's table."[6] The UCC *Book of Worship* makes clear that "the invitation and the call to the supper emphasize that all people of faith are welcome at Christ's Table."[7]

In *The Book of Order,* the Presbyterian Church (U.S.A.) states who is welcome at Christ's Table:

> All the baptized faithful are to be welcomed to the Table, and none shall be excluded because of race, sex, age, economic status, social class, handicapping condition, difference of culture or language, or any barrier created by human injustice. . . . Each time they gather at the Table, the believing community
> - are united with the church in every place, and the whole church is present;
> - join with all the faithful in heaven and on earth in offering thanksgiving to the triune God;
> - renew the vows taken at Baptism;
> and they commit themselves afresh to love and serve God, one another, and their neighbors in the world.[8]

In a booklet written to help parents teach and experience communion with their children, Betty Crowell has said that "communion is a meal of many meanings."[9] As we come to worship and to partake in the communion, we bring with us a lifetime of understandings, experiences, and words to describe this sacrament. It is important to understand two kinds of meanings, those that evolve from our biblical and theological roots, and those that emerge out of our communal experience of Christ's Table. These meanings are not discrete, but rather, taken together, they help us to understand this meal and to share its meanings with the youngest ones in our midst.

Biblical and Theological Meanings

There are four basic meanings of Holy Communion, which together form the liturgy used in celebrating this sacrament: thanksgiving, remembrance, invocation, and communion.

After the words of invitation to the table, the liturgy is focused on the Great Prayer of Thanksgiving. This prayer includes words of thanksgiving and remembrance and an invocation of the Spirit, all in preparation for the "communion of the faithful."[10]

"The eucharist, which always includes both word and sacrament," says the World Council of Churches, "is a proclamation and a celebration of the work of God." [11] We give thanks to God for all that God has done and is doing in the church and in the world.

In Holy Communion we also remember the work of Christ on our behalf. The liturgy helps us remember that "every time we eat this bread and drink this cup, we proclaim the birth, the life, the saving death, and the resurrection of our Lord Jesus Christ until he comes again to establish his realm."[12]

The "Baptism, Eucharist, and Ministry" document of the World Council of Churches notes that this act of remembering Christ's work is "both representation and anticipation. It is not only a calling to mind of what is past and of its significance. It is the Church's effective proclamation of God's mighty acts and promises."[13]

In the last part of the Great Prayer of Thanksgiving, we invoke the presence of the Spirit:

> Eternal God,
> let your Holy Spirit move in power over us
> and over these earthly gifts of bread and wine,
> that they may be the communion of the body and
> blood of Christ,

and that we may become one in him.
May his coming in glory find us
ever watchful in prayer,
strong in truth and love,
and faithful in the breaking of the bread.

Then, at last, all peoples will be free,
all divisions healed,
and with your whole creation,
we will sing your praise,
through your Son, Jesus Christ.[14]

The World Council of Churches asserts that in the confidence of our faith and our relationship with God, we invoke God's Spirit so that the church "may be sanctified and renewed, led into all justice, truth and unity, and empowered to fulfill its mission in the world."[15]

Having given thanks to God, remembered the gracious acts of Christ, and invoked the power of the Spirit, God's people come to communion to "eat the meal which [God] has prepared." We celebrate the meal as God's gift, a gift of power to transform our lives and in turn the world. "The very celebration of the eucharist is an instance of the Church's participation in God's mission to the world. This participation takes everyday form in the proclamation of the Gospel, service of the neighbor, and faithful presence in the world."[16]

Communal Meanings

As we consider the meanings of the sacrament of communion, it is essential to discuss how the four biblical and theological meanings (thanksgiving, remembrance, invocation, and communion) can be communicated to children. Crowell's description of communion, the "meal of many meanings," through six concepts provides a useful way for unlocking the theological significance behind the sacrament.

These six concepts are remembrance, thanksgiving, celebration, forgiveness, being fed and feeding others, and belonging. Crowell's concepts of remembrance (telling the biblical stories of God's acts of love) and thanksgiving correspond to the theological meanings of remembrance and thanksgiving.

Crowell's concept of celebration as an affirmation of God's continued presence calls to mind the act of invoking God's Spirit in our lives. The fourth theological meaning of communion is wonderfully illustrated in Crowell's concepts of forgiveness, being fed and feeding others, and belonging: "As we share in the bread and the wine or grape juice, we are reminded that as our needs for food, for God, for love, are cared for, we are called to offer to others the same care and love that is ours from God. As we are blessed, we are called to be a blessing to others."[17]

In describing the meaning of the sacrament as one of belonging, Crowell affirms the deep relationship between our baptism and our continuing journey as God's faithful people.

Preparing to Come to the Table

I have two good friends, Sarah and Scott, who are Jewish. Friday evening marks the beginning of the Jewish Sabbath (Shabbat). Their observance begins with a celebration and meal in their home, and it then moves to the synagogue for services on Friday evening and again on Saturday. The Shabbat celebration reminds Jewish families to sanctify time and to be aware of God's presence in their lives as they say the blessings, light the candles, drink from the kiddush cup, and share the challah.

From their birth, Jewish children are participants in this ritual. Max, the son of my good friends, was given his own kiddush cup as a gift in honor of his coming into the covenant eight days after his birth. He looks forward to lighting the candles, drinking from his special cup, and eating the challah. (He knows that his family makes two loaves of the twisted bread called challah, one to eat on Friday evening— with something left over for the next day, hopefully —and one loaf to give away to friends.) Some of the first words he learned enabled his participation in this meal: "Shabbat, Shalom," which means "Sabbath peace." Max is being raised with family faith traditions that support the continued growth of his faith and his participation in the congregation's Sabbath worship.

For my friends, the words of Deuteronomy 6:4–9 are living practices. They recite God's words to their children; they discuss them at home and elsewhere. Their faith in God is evident on their hands, on the doorpost of their house (where their mezuzah is nailed), and most of all in their hearts. Their Sabbath celebration moves from their dining room table to their place of worship. There is an explicit connection between their faithful practices at home and their worship in the synagogue.

Consider the preparation that takes place in your home before you go to church. In what ways do you prepare your heart and mind to participate in worship? Do you read scripture, reminding yourself of the words of Jesus regarding the communion? Do you spend time in prayer, remembering the saints who have gone before you and the family and friends with whom you have shared this meal? Do you take time to think about the food that God provides for you, food both literal and symbolic, which nourishes your soul as well as your body?

And what about the children in your house? In what ways do you help prepare them for this meal? Sunday morning may not be the best time for such preparations if your family finds itself in a rush to get up, eat breakfast, dress, and get to church on time. Perhaps Saturday should be the day when preparations begin for the celebration of Holy Communion.

Personal Preparation

Four concepts serve as a framework for family activities designed to connect the meaning of the communion with our preparations for its celebration in worship. These concepts—thanksgiving, remembrance, invocation, and communion—were defined earlier as the four biblical and theological meanings of Holy Communion. Reflecting on these concepts means a commitment to intentionality and ritual.

Consider for a moment your personal preparations for communion. What if the only moments available to you are the two or three minutes of prelude at the beginning of worship? How do you use these moments? Does your preparation include focusing on the meanings of the sacrament for you at this moment in your life?

If we believe that at the table we are reconciled with Christ, then it follows that we must also be reconciled with those around us. Do you prepare to come to the table by reflecting on the conflicts or divisions present in your life, the reconciling work that needs to be done? Joining your family and friends around the Christ's Table requires prayerful, thoughtful, and intentional preparation.

One of the important celebrations of Holy Communion is the first Sunday in October, known as World Communion. On this day, Christians all over the world remember the same words of Jesus, eat bread and drink from a cup, and renew the commitments made during baptism. The ritual of the table is observed in small villages in Africa, congregations in Korea, rural towns in Kansas, and large cities all over this country and the world. Though languages and customs may vary, the ritual is the same.

Just as Jewish families begin their Sabbath preparations at home with time-honored rituals of bread, wine, candles, prayers, and scripture, so we too can acknowledge the place of ritual in our life. Rituals have the power of connection and memory. It is possible, even in lives where time becomes our most precious possession, to ritualize our preparations for communion. Regular moments of preparation can be included in family life, if such moments are deemed important. What do you and your family most need as you prepare to come to Christ's Table?

Preparation at Home

Listed here are a number of ways to prepare for coming to the table. Read over the list and see if one or more of the ideas fits you and your family. These suggestions are designed to illustrate the connection between meanings of and preparation for Holy Communion.

Thanksgiving
1. At lunch or dinner on Sunday, talk about the things you are thankful for.
2. Invite a guest or guests to share in a meal with your family either before or after you come to Christ's Table.

Remembrance
3. Tell the story of Jesus and the disciples in the upper room, or one of the many stories of Jesus sharing a meal with friends.
4. Talk about what happens in the liturgy of communion. This is especially important with younger children. Help them to remember what they are to do during the liturgy.

5. Select a symbol that can be placed on the dining table on days when you have communion at church. What symbol connects this meal with the meal Christ shared with the disciples?

Invocation

6. For a blessing at the lunch or dinner following communion, sing a few verses of the hymn "Let Us Break Bread Together on Our Knees."
7. Have members of the family take turns being responsible for the blessing at each meal, saying a blessing of their own or selecting the one that will be said or sung by everyone.

Communion

8. Volunteer as a family to bake a loaf of bread for the communion table.
9. Bake two loaves of bread, one to have with a meal on Saturday and one to give away to someone in the neighborhood or at church on Sunday.
10. Volunteer as a family to help set the communion table at church. You can then talk with your children about the traditions of your church. Is there a special cloth used on the communion table? What is the story behind the cup, the plate, or the pitcher used for the elements?
11. Practice any responses (spoken or sung) that are used in the communion liturgy.
12. Involve children in helping to clean up after communion. Families or church school classes could take turns volunteering for this duty.

Preparing the Table

A course I teach in seminary focuses on the relevance of the sacraments of baptism and communion in the life of a worshiping community. One of the course requirements is to create a workshop designed to help participants integrate theory, practice, liturgy, and theology. Several years ago two students decided to design a workshop for children and their parents that would help prepare them for communion. Included with the paper they submitted was a small handmade bag containing several wooden objects. On the bag were cutouts of bread and grapes. In the bag was a wooden cup, a small loaf of wooden bread, a round plate, and a white cloth with a small cross stitched in one corner.

A colleague had earlier shared with me a bag of Torah toys he had seen advertised and had purchased to show to his class on the theology of the sacraments. The wooden toys were designed to give Jewish children a chance to gain experience with the rituals of the Shabbat service. Intrigued by the practical nature of hands-on experience with these "toys," I took them to my class and remarked that it would be interesting to have communion toys to help Christian children learn about this sacrament.

The students heard this suggestion and included communion toys with their paper. They had found a member of one of their churches who was a carpenter. They told him what they wanted, and he had made the small loaf of bread with a dowel in the middle, so that children could "break the bread."

After that class ended, I left town to visit friends in Alabama over the Christmas holidays. I took the bag of communion toys with me and showed them to Jonathon, the fourteen-year-old son of my friends. He and his brother worked with their father in his wood shop, and I knew Jonathon might like to see the wooden objects. I showed him the toys and told him how such concrete objects could help children learn about abstract concepts. Jonathon thought the toys were interesting but didn't say a whole lot about them.

A year later when I returned for a visit, Jonathon invited me into the shop at the back of their house. He was the only youth in his church going through confirmation, but he was fortunate to have an elder in the church mentoring him. He had decided that he wanted to make a gift for the congregation on the occasion of his confirmation. His gift was going to be a set of wooden communion pieces, a cup and a loaf of bread. The cup was finished. He handed me the bread, which was a work in progress—he was still making indentations in the wood to simulate the ridges on the top of the bread.

On the day of Jonathon's confirmation, he presented the bread and the cup to the congregation for use in teaching children the meaning of the sacrament of communion.

Coming to the Table

A passage of scripture frequently used as in invitation to Christ's Table is found in Luke 24:30–31. After the Resurrection, Jesus was walking to the village of Emmaus. In the course of the journey he met two men and talked with them about the death of Jesus of Nazareth. It wasn't until they sat down for a meal and Jesus "took bread, blessed and broke it, and gave it to them" that "their eyes were opened, and they recognized him."

We prepare to come to Christ's Table with our heads and our hearts. We come, like the men on the road to Emmaus, with our questions and our wonderings. We come as God's faithful people, intent on living in response to God's gracious acts on our behalf. And in the midst of our musings, our questions, and our preparations, the bread is broken and the cup is poured and our eyes are opened once again—we recognize Jesus, the host at the table.

We prepare our heads and our hearts for that which is most mysterious and least explainable. Yet we seek simplicity in the complexity, and complexity in the simplicity. With all we know as adults, with all our experience, learning, and wisdom, we come to the table in the sure knowledge that "whoever does not receive the dominion of God as a little child will never enter it" (Luke 18:17).

Liturgical and Educational Models

As you think about your congregation's communion liturgy and how children and youth can be prepared for this liturgy, consider using the following models. The first model is fully designed for immediate use, and the other three are outlined so that you can adapt them to your particular setting.

1. "This Bread and This Cup": A Workshop for Children and Parents

This one-and-a-half- to two-hour workshop is designed to teach young children (kindergarten and early elementary age) about the sacrament of communion. Some congregations include children at Christ's Table as early as the age of three or whenever parents choose. Other congregations have a more explicit practice of preparation for first communion at a particular time, such as when a child reaches first grade. Whatever the practice of your congregation, this workshop, if offered once a year, can help children and parents explore the meanings of the sacrament.

Purpose. The purpose of this workshop is to enable younger children and their parents to understand the sacrament of communion and how this meal is celebrated in worship.

Objectives. By the end of the session, learners will have had the opportunity to do the following:

• Identify the meaning of the symbols used in the meal.
• Discuss the different parts of the liturgy.
• Practice singing communion hymns.
• Contribute to the writing of a Great Prayer of Thanksgiving.

Room Setup. The size of the room will depend on the number of participants. The workshop includes both large-group activities in the main section of the room and small-group activities in learning centers. Put up posters or pictures of the sacrament, bread, cup, grapes, and wheat. Have chairs for adults and smaller chairs for children, or quilts on the floor where people can sit. Have a chair and a small table for the teacher. On the table, place a plate and a loaf of bread and a chalice or communion cup filled with juice.

Activities. This workshop requires several older youth and adults to teach and to help with the learning centers. Asking members of the confirmation class to help teach this session is a good way of helping them recall the meaning of the sacrament.

The workshop should include the following activities:

1. *Opening the session* (30 minutes): Welcome the children and their parents as they arrive and ask them to write their name on a name tag. The name tags could already be made in the shape of a loaf of bread or a communion chalice.

Begin by asking the learners to tell the group about celebrations that are special in their family. What does your family do to celebrate a birthday? After the children have shared their stories, ask them what makes these celebrations special. Then tell them that today they will have a chance to learn about a special celebration in the church, one that helps us remember Jesus and what he taught us when he lived on the earth a long time ago.

Teach the group, if they don't already know it, the communion hymn "Let Us Break Bread Together on Our Knees." If the hymn is already familiar to the group, try signing it as you sing it.

Spend some time learning what the children have already observed about the sacrament, and the meanings they have understood. Questions such as these will fuel this discussion:

- Once a month in our church (or however often the sacrament is observed), we do something special in worship. What is it we do?
- Why do you think we do this?
- What is different about the service?
- What do you notice on the communion table?
- Why do we have bread and juice?
- Do you remember any of the words that the minister says? If so, what do you remember?

Then tell the story of the Last Supper in your own words, based on the account in either Matthew or Luke. Have a Bible on your lap and tell the children that the story comes from the New Testament. As you tell the story, be sure to allow time for questions and responses.

Also talk about the different words used in talking about the sacrament: Christ's Table, the meal, the communion, the eucharist. Explain what each of these words mean. Affirm that we participate in this sacrament because

- Jesus wanted us to remember him and what he said;
- Jesus left us the signs of bread and juice; and
- when we eat the bread and drink the juice, we remember Jesus.

Explaining the meaning of the sacrament to the children is an excellent way for youth and adults to interpret the meaning for themselves.

Then describe the learning centers and invite the children and their parents to decide which ones they want to work in. Be sure to have leaders available in each of the centers. This design assumes a group of at least eight or more children and their parent or parents. If your group is smaller, decide which of the centers you would like to include. You could offer them as options or do several of the learning activities together as a group.

2. *Developing the session* (45–60 minutes): The following learning centers can be set up around the room.

- Design a Bulletin Cover: Have paper, crayons, and markers available for participants to design bulletin covers related to communion. Along with the art supplies, have pictures of Bible stories showing Jesus eating with people, pictures of the Last Supper, and pictures of bread and grapes. Also have a bowl of grapes and a loaf of bread present.
- Make a Place mat: Have construction paper, scissors, glue, crayons, and markers available. Invite children to draw a picture that they could use for a place mat at home. You could have communion symbols already cut out of construction paper for those who need help in getting started. After a learner has finished a picture, have clear contact paper available to use in covering both sides of the picture. Backing the picture with a sheet of cardboard (or drawing directly on cardboard) makes the place mat more sturdy.
- Say Thank You to God: Before we eat the communion meal, we say thank you to God. This important part of the service is called the Great Prayer of Thanksgiving. It follows a simple form. Read over examples of the prayer in your church's book of worship. Involve the learners in the writing of a prayer of thanksgiving using the following outline:

Thanksgiving—Ask participants to think of why they are thankful to God. ("We thank you God for . . .")

Remembrance—Encourage learners to recall stories from the Bible about God and God's creation. ("When we think about you, O God, we remember . . .")

Offering—Think of ways to offer God praise and thanksgiving. What are some ways that we can offer our very selves to God?

Memorial Acclamation—Recall stories of Jesus and his ministry, teaching, sacrifice, and resurrection.

Invocation of the Spirit—Affirm the presence of God's Spirit with God's people in all times and places.

Doxology—End the prayer in praise to God, who is Creator, Redeemer, and Spirit.

• Celebrate with a Banner: Have a large piece of paper spread on the floor or taped to the wall. Across the top of the paper, write the words *WE CELEBRATE*. Ask the learners to draw pictures that tell about celebrations important in their family.

• Read a Book Together: Have a book center available for those who would like to read or hear a story about Jesus eating with people. You can use some of the books mentioned here or have Bible storybooks, such as the *Arch Books* series, available.

• Visit the Sanctuary: Have a person lead the learners into the sanctuary to talk about the meal and how it is served in your congregation. Have bread and a chalice on the table. Invite the children to ask questions and share observations. Talk about the different ways that communion is served and about who prepares the bread and the cup for communion.

• Make Communion Bread: Set up a table in the room (or in the kitchen, if it is nearby) so that learners can help make bread together. Some could help mix the ingredients. Others could knead dough that had been prepared in advance and had already gone through one rising. Still others could help put risen dough in the oven and baste it with butter or an egg white before it cooks. Make sure the finished bread is used at the next communion.

3. *Concluding the session* (15–30 minutes): You can conclude your time together in several ways. One would be to retell the story of Jesus in the upper room with the disciples—see if the children can help you tell the story. You could also read Paul's account of this story in 1 Corinthians 11:23–26. As you read the story, stop and ask the children these questions:

How did Paul learn about the supper?
When was the first time this meal took place?
What is the symbol for Christ's body? Christ's blood?
Why does Jesus want us to eat this meal and remember this time?
What does Paul say we are doing every time we eat this meal together?[18]

You could also conclude by reading a short children's book about communion, such as Jeanne S. Fogle's *Signs of God's Love: Baptism and Communion* (Philadelphia: Geneva Press, 1984) or John M. Barrett's *Big in God's Eyes: A Story about Children and Communion* (New York: United Church Press, 1985).

Have bread and grapes for everyone to share. If the group has written a Great Prayer of Thanksgiving, use it to conclude the workshop.

2. *"This Meal We Eat": A Class for Parents of Young Children*

Some congregations encourage parents to bring their child to communion any time after baptism. Other congregations assume that all persons are welcome at the table at any time. Still other churches have a tradition of first communion; coming to the table is tied to a particular event, such as entering first grade. Congregational practices are usually related to polity and theology, but they are also based on context and tradition.

The design for this class for parents assumes a congregation that welcomes children to the table at any time. This practice encourages parents to be a partner with the church in nurturing their child's growth in faith and in understanding of the sacrament. Some parents feel quite comfortable in this role. Others feel less comfortable because they have not explored the meanings of communion for themselves.

The class is divided into four one-hour sessions. It is appropriate for parents of children three to seven years of age. Children of this age are beginning to come to worship (or parts of worship) and are able to articulate their questions about the service.

Purpose. The purpose of this class is to encourage parents of young children in exploring the meanings of the sacrament of communion and to help them in identifying practical ways to nurture their children's understanding of the sacrament.

Setting. The class could meet in the church during church school, in a home, or at a retreat location.

Session One: "Holy Communion: Experiences and Meanings"

Objectives. By the end of this session, learners will have had the opportunity to do the following:

- Share experiences and understandings of communion.
- Identify areas of misunderstanding or confusion.
- Become familiar with denominational and congregational traditions and theology regarding communion, learning the beliefs all Christians hold in common and the ways your congregation is unique in its celebration of this sacrament.

Session Two: "The Liturgy for Communion"

Objectives. By the end of this session, learners will have had the opportunity to do the following:

- Identify the parts of the liturgy of communion: what we affirm, what we pray, what we sing, what we do.
- Discuss the meaning of the different parts of the liturgy.
- Discuss the theology of the sacrament by looking at a variety of communion hymns.

Session Three: "What a Child Brings to the Table"

Objectives. By the end of this session, learners will have had the opportunity to do the following:

- Discuss the meanings of the sacrament that a child can understand.
- Identify reasons why children are included and welcomed at the table.

Session Four: "The Partnership of Home and Church"

Objectives. By the end of this session, learners will have had the opportunity to do the following:

- Discuss the ways parents can help prepare their children for communion.
- Identify books and resources that teach about the sacrament.
- Share ideas for connecting the dining table at home with Christ's table at church.

Activities. From the following list of activities, choose those that best fit your congregation:

1. View and discuss a video that teaches about the sacrament. Some possibilities are as follows:

• *In Remembrance,* the story of the Last Supper. Available from
Ecufilm (47 minutes; call 1-800-251-4091).
• *The Meaning of Mystery: The Sacraments of the Church,* from a
Reformed perspective. Available from Presbyterian Publishing
House (two 20-minute segments, including a user's guide; call
1-800-227-2872).

2. Examine worship bulletins from a communion service and discuss the different parts of the liturgy from the perspective of your faith
tradition. What ways of celebrating the sacrament are unique to this
particular congregation? What other traditions have been experienced
by members of the class?

3. Use material from the earlier part of this chapter for background
in discussing the theological meanings of the sacrament. Essential to
this discussion is the contrast between the sacrament as a memorial
and the sacrament as a celebration.

4. Sing and discuss the meaning of a variety of communion hymns
found in your hymnbook. What is being communicated about the
sacrament through the words and the music? Some hymns you could
look at are listed here. They can be found in the following hymnbooks:
The New Century Hymnal (United Church of Christ); *The Chalice
Hymnal* (Disciples of Christ); *The Presbyterian Hymnal*; and Ruth
Duck's *Dancing in the Universe: Hymns and Songs* (Chicago: GIA
Publications, 1992).

> "We Come as Guests Invited" (words by Timothy Dudley-Smith)
> "Una Espiga" (Sheaves of Summer; words by Cesareo Gabarain)
> "Come, Risen Lord" (words by George W. Briggs)
> "Be Known to Us in Breaking Bread" (words by James Mont-
> gomery)
> "In Remembrance of Me" (words by Ragan Courtney)
> "Take Our Bread" (words by Joe Wise)
> "Lord, We Have Come at Your Own Invitation" (words by Fred
> Pratt Green)
> "Jesus Thou Joy of Loving Hearts" (words by Bernard of Clair-
> vaux)
> "I Come with Joy" (words by Brian Wren)
> "Let Us Talents and Tongues Employ" (words by Fred Kaan)

"You Satisfy the Hungry Heart" (words by Omer Westendorf)
"Jesus Took the Bread" (words by Ruth C. Duck)
"Deck Yourself, My Soul, with Gladness" (words by Johann Franck)

5. With the help of a minister, examine the parts of the Great Prayer of Thanksgiving. Have different examples of this prayer available for people to look at. Involve the group in trying to write a simple prayer using the following form:

Thanksgiving
Remembrance
Offering
Memorial Acclamation
Invocation of the Spirit
Doxology

6. Provide time for sharing experiences of the sacrament at places other than in this congregation. What meanings of the sacrament are most important in your life?

7. Discuss together how to explain the sacrament and its meanings to young children.

8. Read and discuss parts of one of the following books that relate to the sacrament of communion:

- Leonardo Boff, *Sacraments of the Life, Life of the Sacraments* (Washington, D.C.: Pastoral Press, 1987).
- John Burkhart, *Worship* (Louisville: Westminster Press, 1982).
- "Eucharist," in "Baptism, Eucharist, and Ministry" Faith and Order Paper no. 111 (Geneva: World Council of Churches, 1982).
- Sara Covin Juengst, *Breaking Bread: The Spiritual Significance of Food* (Louisville: Westminster John Knox, 1992).
- John Poulton, *The Feast of Life: A Theological Reflection on the Theme Jesus Christ, the Life of the World* (Geneva: World Council of Churches, 1982).
- William Willimon, *Sunday Dinner: The Lord's Supper and the Christian Life* (Nashville: Upper Room, 1981).

9. Discuss the different ways that the sacrament is served—seated, by intinction, with a common cup—and the meanings behind these

practices. This discussion could also include an exploration of the differences in tradition that keep Christians divided at the table. The group could then choose another church in the community to approach about celebrating the sacrament together on World Communion Sunday.

10. Have a meal together to conclude the sessions. Invite each family represented to bring a loaf of bread to the meal, either one they have baked or one they have bought; emphasize that either kind of bread is welcome at the table. Have a simple meal of soup, salad, and bread, and share insights from the class.

3. "Special Times with Children": Worship on Communion Sunday

Setting aside a moment for children during worship gives a lay person or the minister a chance to directly address children of preschool and younger elementary ages. The names given to these moments are as varied as our congregations: Children's Sermon, Church Talk, A Time for Children, and so forth. The usual format begins with a biblical story, followed by a talk together and a brief prayer. The setting is usually early in the worship service, at the front of the sanctuary with children gathered around the person who is leading the moment.

Such moments work when the concept being communicated is appropriate for the children's level of thinking and interaction. They do not work when the teaching is too abstract for children's concrete level of thinking, or when the moral lessons offered are beyond the comprehension of the children.

Here are some themes that could be used with children on Sundays when communion is celebrated. Because children learn best when more than one of their senses is involved, suggestions are given for a symbol that can be used to illustrate key concepts.

1. *Sharing a Meal:* Tell the story of the feeding of the five thousand made possible because a child shared a lunch of loaves and fishes. Symbol: a basket containing small loaves of bread and fish cut out of paper or fabric.

2. *The Meal in the Upper Room:* Tell the story of the Passover meal. Talk about why we still eat this meal today. Symbol: a basket with bread and grapes.

3. *Table Symbols:* With the chalice and the plate as symbols, talk about why Jesus used these particular elements.

4. *The World Table:* For World Communion Sunday, fill a basket with a variety of breads: pita, herb, multigrain, matzo. Talk about the different kinds of bread and relate this discussion to Christians all over the world coming to the table on this day to break bread and drink from the cup. Explain that the table unites us with Christians all over the world.

5. *Singing a Hymn:* Teach the children the communion hymn "Let Us Break Bread Together on Our Knees." If there is someone who can teach the children to sign the hymn, have this person do so. Then let the children invite the congregation to join them in singing this hymn as a preparation for coming to the table.

6. *An Important Story:* Use Jeanne S. Fogle's *Signs of God's Love: Baptism and Communion* to talk with the children about the story behind the meal at the table. Begin with questions to help them state what they know and understand.

7. *Giving Thanks:* Using the form for the Great Prayer of Thanksgiving suggested in this chapter, invite the children to write a prayer and then use it in the liturgy.

8. *Talking about Bread:* Talk about how bread is made and why we eat it. Ask the children why they think Jesus chose bread to symbolize his love for everyone. Symbol: a basket of bread.

4. "Coming to the Table": Suggestions for a Child-Friendly Communion

If your church is willing to look at communion from the perspective of younger participants, you could invite members of the Christian Education Committee to meet with members of the Worship Committee to discuss some of the suggestions that follow. Look over the suggestions in advance and decide which ones are most pertinent to your congregation.

The committees should first assess how child-friendly your congregation is. What is your church saying and doing that explicitly welcomes the presence, participation, and leadership of children and youth? What are the implicit messages and traditions? What is missing in your church that could be added to enable the participation of all baptized children?

In particular, the committees should examine the following aspects of the communion service:

1. *The worship bulletin.* Worship services are usually planned with adult participants in mind. It is implicit that children and youth simply fit in as they are able and interested. Look over a worship bulletin from a Sunday when Holy Communion is included. Read the bulletin through the eyes of a five-year-old, an eight-year-old, and a thirteen-year-old. What in this service encourages their interest and their participation?

2. *The liturgy.* What hymns are sung? What prayers are used? What responses are included? Are these responses printed? Can they be easily learned by even the youngest members of the church?

3. *The communion process.* How are the bread and the cup given to the congregation? Are trays passed to people in pews? Is communion served by intinction, with everyone who is able coming forward to tear off a piece of bread and then dipping it in the cup? Are even the youngest ones in your midst encouraged to participate, or are they hindered in some way? Some congregations have a tradition of holding the bread and the cup until all have been served, and then eating and drinking together as one. It is a wonderful symbol, rich in theological and ecclesiological significance, but have you ever watched an active and inquisitive four year old try to hold a small cup of juice?

If the elements are served to the congregation as they are seated, are people encouraged to say to each other, "This is the body of Christ" or "This is the bread of life" and "This is the cup of the new covenant"? A simple communion greeting to a child is, "Mary Elizabeth, God loves you." The congregation where I worship has a tradition of wearing name tags on communion Sunday. When we pass the elements to each other, we can call each person by name.

We Come as Guests Invited

*"Come to me all you that are weary and carrying heavy burdens, and I will give you rest." —*Matt. 11:28

"I am the bread of life. Whoever comes to me will never be hungry, and whoever believes in me will never be thirsty."
*—*John 6:35

The third verse of the hymn "We Come as Guests Invited" (words by Timothy Dudley-Smith) begins this way:

One bread is ours for sharing,
One single fruitful vine.
Our fellowship declaring
Renewed in bread and wine:
Renewed, sustained, and given
By token, sign, and word,
The pledge and seal of heaven,
The love of Christ our Lord.

The use of the word *one* in this hymn is a reminder of the unity expressed in the coming together to Christ's Table. As Jesus shared the loaf of bread and the one cup with his disciples, so we come to one table to share the loaf and the cup. We come from different families and different churches and different countries to the one table. We come, leaving behind differences of age, race, class, and gender, to unite together in Christian fellowship and to eat the meal that renews and sustains us.

It is difficult to imagine the unity and oneness represented in the symbols of the meal without children at the table. Having been welcomed with water into the life of a congregation, the presence of children reminds us of the promises we made at their baptisms. Every time we eat the bread and drink from the cup, we know that we are joined with them in telling the stories of Jesus and living the faith to which we are called.

Another communion hymn, "You Satisfy the Hungry Heart" (words by Omer Westendorf), concludes with this verse:

You give yourself to us, O Lord;
Then selfless let us be.
To serve each other in your name,
In truth and charity

We come to the table as invited guests, and we leave with our hearts full and satisfied. This joyful feast is a visible reminder that all of God's children are welcome at the table.

Participation in this meal also satisfies our hunger to understand the mystery that is God. For a brief sacramental moment, we are invited into God's presence, God's covenanting relationship. Leonardo Boff has spoken of the power of the sacrament in our lives: "A sacrament does not tear human beings away from this world. It addresses an appeal to them, asking them to look more closely and deeply into the very heart of the world. . . . The essential vocation of human beings on earth is to become sacramental human beings."[19] The power of the mystery moves with us as we leave the table and move out into the world.

Jesus said, "Come unto me." And so we come to the table to eat the bread and drink from the cup of the new covenant, symbols of God's eternal love and presence in the lives of God's creation. We come unto the one whose food always satisfies, the one, eternal God who empowers us to be "sacramental human beings."

5 Moving from the Table

Alarm clocks weren't needed to wake this family. The family dog, looking for someone to let her outside and feed her, found an arm hanging over the edge of the bed and began to lick. Soon after, the two year old ran from his bed to join his parents for an early morning snuggle. Another day had begun. But it wasn't just another day for this family, it was Sunday. The children knew this because Saturday night meant washing hair before bedtime and reminders from their parents that "Tomorrow is church day!"

Slowly, the rest of the house awakened. As preparation for breakfast began, children found a few minutes to play with their toys. The oldest child got the watering can and began to water the houseplants, something he did every week at this time. As he was watering the African violet in the living room, he noticed buds appearing from among the leaves, and he ran to tell his mother that soon it would be blooming. She went with him to see this new growth and thanked him for his loving care of the houseplants.

As the smell of toast and coffee began to fill the kitchen, the father heard his middle child call him to come quickly. He ran into the next room and asked his daughter what was wrong. She told him to look into the fish tank. One of their goldfish had died. They had three goldfish in the tank, one for each child. She looked at the markings on the fish and realized it was the one that her baby sister had named. "It's my sister's fish, she named it Orange because of its color. Can we get her another one?" Her father assured her that they would. What about Orange? "We'll need to bury her," her father said. They could do it after they got home from church. They would find a nice place outside, and they would have a funeral. "What's a funeral?" she asked. Her daddy explained that at a funeral, you have a prayer, sing a song, say something nice about the person or animal who has died, and give thanks to God. Then they would put Orange in the ground. The daughter thought that would be a fine idea, and she wanted to help with the funeral.

Breakfast was ready, and everyone gathered at the table to eat together. It was the two year old's turn to select the blessing to sing before the meal. She announced she wanted to sing, "For health and strength and daily food, we give you thanks O God." As they held hands around the table, everyone joined her in singing the blessing.

They talked about going to church and how today would be communion Sunday. The oldest child would be staying with his parents during worship. His younger sisters would leave worship to go to an extended session after the special time for children. He was glad he was big enough to stay with his parents, even though sometimes it was hard to sit still and stay quiet for so long.

He liked communion Sundays. There were more things to do and watch. The part he liked best was getting to walk with his parents to the front of the church and tear off a piece of bread and dip it in the cup. He liked the way the minister looked right at him and called him by name and said, "This is the bread of life which is for you." Then he moved to the person holding the cup—it was his church school teacher, Jeff, who held the cup down so he could reach it and said, "This is the cup of the new covenant." He didn't really know what *covenant* meant, but he did know this was a special time, a time when he could remember Jesus and his life and death and his sharing of this meal with the disciples. When he ate this meal (which he thought really wasn't a very big meal, more like a snack), it made him think that maybe he too was one of Jesus' disciples.

While they were finishing their breakfast, they heard a knock at the door. When it was opened, they saw their neighbor, Nancy, standing there. Nancy was not only a neighbor, she was a friend to everyone in the family. Nancy was in her seventies and lived by herself. She loved inviting the children to her house to visit, help water her plants, and share in a special afternoon treat of freshly baked chocolate chip cookies. Nancy said that she needed some help and wondered if after church someone could come over. She needed to move some furniture around, and she couldn't do it by herself. They said, of course, they would be glad to help, and they invited her to join them for lunch after they got home from church. She said that would be wonderful. She ate so many meals by herself; she loved to share a meal with others.

After finishing breakfast, everyone left the table to get dressed for church. They got there a few minutes late, but that was normal for this family. They never knew what would happen first thing in the morning, especially on Sundays. As they sat together in worship listening to the minister begin the liturgy for communion, they heard the words from Luke about Jesus meeting the disciples on the road to Emmaus. The disciples had not recognized Jesus until they sat down together at a table for a meal together. The parents looked at each other and smiled and thought about the many ways they recognized Jesus every day in their lives. They wondered about the many ways they would be challenged this week to be disciples. They wondered what they would be called to do, and if they would be ready to respond.

Meanings and Movements

Day by day, attending the temple together and breaking bread in their homes, they partook of food with glad and generous hearts.   —Acts 2:46

The Gospels tell of the awakening of a culture to a new way of thinking and acting. The words and actions of Jesus were often misunderstood, challenged by authorities, feared as revolutionary, but passionately believed by many people of all ages.

The writer of Acts records the story of the earliest Christian communities as they struggled to live as a minority group of faithful followers of the one they believed to be the Messiah. Living and worshiping as a countercultural group, they sought ways to remember the faith they had been taught and to rehearse together their call to live in the larger world.

The story of the first Christians is our story today. To think that Christians are a majority in any culture is to live in delusion. To think that most societal institutions support and affirm Christian values is folly. It is time to rethink our identity and calling as Christians, as disciples of Jesus Christ. We are called in these last years of the twentieth century to live with intentionality.

It is time to rethink the ways we come to the table and move out from it into the world. We are helped in this task if we rethink the meal itself, the meal we call Holy Communion, the Eucharist. William Willimon says that he "grieves that our Sunday services seem more like memorials of God's absence rather than celebrations of God's presence."[1] Our world is in desperate need of Christians who can leave the table in worship and affirm with hope and commitment the places where God is present and working in the world.

The table serves as a useful metaphor for both the reality and the vision of our task as Christians living as a minority in our culture. The image of a table also serves to connect the everydayness of our lives with the holiness and mystery of the sacrament. Let's begin by looking at the tables in our homes.

People used to gather at tables for meals, for conversation, for sharing the intimacies and intricacies of daily life. Mealtimes were once occasions when families came together not only to share a meal, but to share the events of the day. Unfortunately, such family gatherings are becoming increasingly rare. Willimon notes the "disintegration of table fellowship," which he relates to the "dissolution of the family."[2] The schedules of each member of the family become a priority over and against spending time together. The culture that used to protect family time now works against it. T-ball games at dinnertime, soccer practices on Sunday mornings, breakfast meetings with clients all work against families trying to break bread together. What is the relationship between this broken table fellowship at home and the act of coming to and moving from the table in worship?

In earlier parts of this century, family meals were also times of family devotions. A former student once told me that devotions in her family took place at mealtime. She remembered learning geography during those times as well; the family devotions focused on what was going on in the world. To aid in their discussion and prayers, a map of the world was attached to the window shade, which was pulled down during the meal. She was formed in her faith in memorable ways.

Such intentional Christian nurture at the table is even more essential today in a culture that Ellen Charry says "shapes children for a world shorn of God."[3] She goes on to say that the church is perhaps the only institution with the beliefs, literature, liturgy, practices, social structure and authority (diminished though it may be) necessary to rescue children from the violence and other deforming features of late 20th-century life. But it cannot accomplish this by simply laying the faith before young people and inviting them to choose it. Nor can it impose Christian identity by force and indoctrination. It can only prepare the setting for the Holy Spirit slowly to nurture children in the Christian faith and practice.[4]

Families and congregations that prepare for and engage in table fellowship at home and in worship are choosing by their actions to make an intentional commitment to Christian nurture. Families that make table fellowship a priority are ensuring that their children will not grow up in a world "shorn of God."

Families and congregations that help interpret events in the world in light of the Gospel of Jesus Christ are helping God's Spirit to work. Congregations that welcome all God's people to Christ's Table and educate them about its power, mystery, and potential equip these people to move from the table and engage in ministry in the world.

There is a liturgical rhythm that moves us from our home table to the communion table. At both tables, we remember family stories, we give thanks for food and nourishment, we claim God's presence, we eat together. In all of these activities we proclaim who we are as Christians and help form the world as God intends it to be.[5] These table activities have the power to form and transform us. Such forming and transforming is essential in our culture.

In commenting on the necessity of allowing baptized children at Christ's Table, Willimon affirms the power of practice. "From our youngest years, we start forming the habits of discipleship. From our first sputtering emergence from the baptismal font, we start learning to confess, forgive, reach out, face the truth, be converted, be fed."[6]

Both tables—at home and at church—contribute to "habits of discipleship," which provide meaning, direction, and power to lives that must be lived in opposition to cultural norms and values. Together we support and nurture each other in the movement from baptismal font to Christ's Table. We affirm that there is no one too young or too old for such rehearsals of living as God intends us to live in the world.

Liturgical and Daily Rhythms

I have a favorite hymn I like to use when planning the liturgy for communion. It captures for me the movement, rhythm, and theology of the meal. It also makes explicit, in a fairly simple way, the implicit meanings of the sacrament. As you read over the verses, notice the verbs used by the hymn writer Fred Kaan.

Let Us Talents and Tongues Employ

Let us talents and tongues employ,
Reaching out with a shout of joy:
Bread is broken, the wine is poured,
Christ is spoken and seen and heard.

Refrain:
Jesus lives again, earth can breathe again,
Pass the Word around: loaves abound!

Christ is able to make us one,
At the table He sets the tone.
Teaching people to live to bless,
Love in word and in deed express.

Jesus calls us in, sends us out
Bearing fruit in a world of doubt,
Gives us love to tell, bread to share:
God (Immanuel) everywhere![7]

There is great energy expressed in this hymn. This energy is furthered by the tune, which Doreen Potter adapted from a Jamaican folk melody. The activity of breaking bread and pouring wine is inextricably woven with specific actions. Every time we prepare to come to the table, we know that at the meal, "Christ is spoken and seen and heard." We are involved in retelling this old, old, story using our talents and tongues.

At the table, as we are ready to receive the bread and the cup, Christ "sets the tone." Christ "make[s] us one," helping us see the ways we need to bless each other and love each other in word and deed.

And finally, Christ's call to the table reminds us of our baptism and "sends us out" to bear fruit, share bread, proclaim to a doubting world that God is alive: "God (Immanuel) everywhere!"

As we prepare to come to the table, as we share in the meal that nourishes our souls, and as we move out into the world in our journeys of faith, we affirm with Christians of all ages and in all times and places a timeless statement of faith: "Jesus lives again, / earth can breathe again, / pass the Word around: loaves abound!"

The sacramental rhythms of breaking bread and pouring the cup are needed in the daily rhythms of our lives. The sacrament of communion reminds us that we need to continue to "pass the Word around," that Jesus is alive, and that "loaves abound," enough for all as we "breathe again" with the earth and all its inhabitants.

There are five theological themes in the eucharistic prayer, or Great Prayer of Thanksgiving, which is a central part of the communion liturgy.[8] These themes also have potential meaning in the daily rhythms of our life. If we are to reach out to a world in doubt, we need to connect the mystery, awe, and wonder of sacramental moments with the possibility of seeing and living sacramentally in our daily lives. In what ways are you already involved in connecting these activities in your life?

1. Giving Thanks

I learned about teaching in the church by going with my sister on Saturday mornings to help my mother set up her church school room for a class of three year olds. It was a ritual for us. We set up the learning centers: blocks, books, nature, worship, art, and music. Pictures were carefully placed at the eye level of preschool children. The teaching theme for the day was carefully printed and posted outside the door at the eye level of adults. Everything in the room was designed to invite the curiosity and learning of young children.

Occasionally I would help out in the classroom, and it was there I learned about giving thanks to God. I watched my mother as we took the children on a nature walk around the church, looking for signs of God's creation. A spider's web, a magnolia seed pod, a butterfly, a leaf changing from green to red, all were evidence of God's creative activity in the world. And usually upon finding these signs, my mother would comment on the beauty and say, "Thank you God, for this beautiful day and everything you have made."

It was a simple prayer of thanksgiving, simple yet concrete. I grew up knowing the interconnectedness of all life. Working in her flower beds, my mother still celebrates each time she finds a large, wiggly earthworm. She taught us how thankful we should be to find earthworms because they were natural aerators of the soil. "God gives us earthworms," she would tell us.

Ruth Duck reminds us that communion "is a meal of thanksgiving in which we give thanks for the presence of Jesus the Christ not only at the table, but in our daily lives with their joy and trouble."[9] How can we come to a meal at the communion table unless we are actively aware and explicit about being thankful in our daily lives? The meal at the table of Jesus Christ and the meals at our home tables share a rhythm of meaning and action, but this connection can be made only if we are active participants at both. Janet Fishburn notes the power of this connection: "The Christian way of ordering life through liturgy is not likely to establish the themes and rhythms of the lives of members unless they are in the habit of regular worship. Members who worship sporadically are much less likely to be able to see the world in a new way, given the power of intellectual, moral and social values of the world in which they live most of their lives."[10]

Faithful Jewish families mark the beginning of their Sabbath with a Shabbat service in their homes on Friday evening. Knowing they are a minority within the culture, they have to keep their faith alive through a commitment to faithful practices at home. Christians would do well to learn from our Jewish friends that the practice of giving thanks to God begins at home and moves with us as we join in worship with our congregation, saying together the familiar words of the communion liturgy:

> God be with you.
> *And also with you.*
> Lift up your hearts.
> *We lift them to God.*
> Let us give thanks to God Most High.
> *It is right to give God thanks and praise.*

2. Remembering

The words spoken at the table are forever etched in our memories. Jesus said, "When you do this, remember me." Whenever we come to the table and eat the bread and drink from the cup, we remember and retell the story of Jesus' birth, life, saving death, and resurrection. And we retell these stories in anticipation of the day when the realm of God will be fulfilled.

Like many other children, I grew up with a Bible storybook that I kept on the table by my bed. After I learned to read, this book became a faithful companion for me before I went to sleep each night. The book contained a few color pictures of biblical characters, but mostly it contained stories from the Bible. Biblical characters, such as Hannah, Samuel, Mary, and Zaccheus, came alive in my imagination as I read and reread the book.

In a time of increasing reliance on technology, it is important to recover the old yet important form of communication called storytelling. A Bible story imaginatively told can capture the attention of a child in a more personal way than the same story told by a television cartoon or a computer program. Telling the stories of Jesus sharing meals with people connects us to our own times of table fellowship at home and in worship.

Think for a moment of your own repertoire of Bible stories. What is in your memory bank? Often I think we fail to pass on the faith stories because we don't know them ourselves, and not wanting to make mistakes, we do nothing. Telling and learning stories and songs about the Bible enables our participation in the teaching and worship life of our congregations. It helps us to continue to tell the old, old, story that is ever new.

The Great Prayer of Thanksgiving used in the liturgy of communion takes a variety of forms in the denominational books of worship. The biblical story is often adapted in this prayer for use in the different seasons of the church year. An important part of the prayer recounts the acts of God as Creator, Redeemer, and Spirit. I have often thought it would be interesting at this point in worship to spontaneously tell the story out of our own memories.

There is power in remembering and telling. Fishburn has noted the importance of the liturgies of the Word and Holy Communion for a congregation when she says that they are forms "through which the Spirit can breathe new life into the people of God. The repetition of prayer, Scripture, hymns, and sacraments over a lifetime—or some part of it—can take root in the heart. The words, the music, a particular way of seeing the world can become part of the life of a congregation."[11]

Remembering our story as the people of God is as important as remembering our family stories. Letting biblical stories "take root in the heart" is one way to form habits of discipleship that enable our formation as members of the family we call Christian. Such a formative activity of remembering is over only when our lives on this earth are finished.

3. Blessing and Invocation

The blessing at the end of worship, just prior to the benediction, has always held special meaning for me. I wait eagerly to hear what the minister will say. How will she send me from this service? How will he weave together the themes of the worship as he sends me out into the world, blessed for service in God's name? When leading worship myself, I most often do not plan what I will say for the blessing. Invoking the presence of God's Spirit, I know that at that moment in the liturgy, the right words of blessing for all God's people will be articulated.

When I worked with local congregations as a church educator, many of the Protestant churches in the community participated in a cooperative campus ministry at the local university. One of the programs sponsored by this ministry was a once-a-week lunch called Horizons. It involved a meal and a brief program for students, administrators, faculty members, and church and community folk.

The meal was prepared and served by the congregations participating in the ministry. Each Tuesday at noon, the meal began with a prayer. After the program was finished and announcements had been made, the campus minister concluded the time with a blessing. It has been twelve years since I was a participant in those gatherings, and I still remember my colleague raising his hand and offering a blessing for those of us gathered together at a common table. I looked forward to this moment of midweek blessing. It nourished me and sustained me in ways as essential as the meal served by the volunteers.

In a blessing, we invoke God's Spirit. We ask for God's presence, knowing that such presence is a transforming gift of God, given freely without measure. It is not something we earn. In commenting on this activity of invocation of the Spirit, or *epiklesis,* Ruth Duck has said that "transformation happens not because of human words or actions alone, but because of the Spirit's work in the church and the world, transforming lives and relationships."[12]

Charry observes that "one also learns to pray by being prayed for. Parents would do well to bless their children, perhaps when they leave for school in the morning, and to pray for them when they are facing special stresses, and at times of celebration."[13] She goes on to note that in order to give this blessing, parents must feel at home with prayer, "comfortable praying aloud and spontaneously—a daunting thought for those accustomed to having the minister do the praying."[14]

Giving and receiving blessings can be a daily activity of invoking God's presence in our lives. Think of the people who bless you with their presence, their hugs, their words of appreciation, their prayers for your health. Consider also the people who need a blessing from you: an elderly member of your family or church, a child in need of someone to talk to or hold on to, a teenager on the way to a work camp, a child leaving home for the first time for summer camp.

Blessing someone in God's name is a simple act that anyone can do. It doesn't take a seminary degree or years of pastoral experience. The more common the activity of blessing becomes, the more we will be able to see and live sacramentally in our daily lives.

4. Eating Together

Once I understood the seasons of the liturgical year, I became convinced of their potential power for connecting the sacred and the secular. The rhythms of the church year gave meaning to life and work, providing balance and encouraging a commitment to Sabbath time and the need for attention to *kairos* (spirit time) as well as *chronos* (clock time).

A group of friends in one of the congregations where I worked formed an Advent lunch group one year. We agreed to meet on the four Sundays of Advent to share in a brief worship service and a sim-

ple lunch after church. We rotated among the homes of the participants. I made copies of simple forms for Advent worship, and we
gathered around the Advent wreath. Different members of the host's
family were responsible for the different parts of the service. Each
host worked intentionally on the Advent service, trying to include single persons as well as their family members in the leadership of the
service. Children in these families grew up participating in the liturgy
of these Advent lunches.

I stayed in this Advent lunch group for eight years and even returned to join the group on the fourth Sunday of Advent for a number
of years after I had moved away to Chicago. During these years of eating together, we watched children grow up, go to college, return home
for the holidays. Extended family members often joined us, as did visitors. New people were invited every year. We represented age groups
all across the lifespan. Usually, on one of the Sundays, a group picture
was taken, and everyone was given a copy.

We need to create times of table fellowship, occasions of being together as family and as friends. The memory of those Advent lunches
is still powerful many years later because it reminds me of the transforming power of eating together. At Christ's Table, we come as individuals but we commune together. Paul reminds us in 1 Cor. 10:17 that
"because there is one bread, we who are many are one body, for we all
partake of the one bread." Ruth Duck adds that "those who share the
meal are being formed into one community in all our diversity."[15]

I now share a Thanksgiving table that is truly multicultural and
multifaith. We come from different faith traditions, family traditions,
and cultural backgrounds to give thanks for food and faith and friendship. My friend and colleague Heidi Hadsell invites us to come and
bring food that is traditional to our own Thanksgiving tables. And so
we come in all our diversity, bringing something that is familiar and
known to a table that is always new. We struggle to hear each other
speak in different languages as we share stories of thanksgiving traditions we have experienced. In the time of gathering, standing in the
kitchen preparing food, and coming to the table, we form for this one
day a new community of God's faithful people.

Participating in these agape table meals over the years with friends
in Alabama and friends in Chicago, I have experienced the power of

hospitality in welcoming the stranger to the table. It reminds me that at the table where Jesus Christ is the host, all are welcome—strangers become friends.

5. A Rehearsal of the World as God Intends It to Be

I choose to live in the city of Chicago for many reasons. A major one is to be near to work. Being in the city also allows me to live among cultural and ethnic diversity and to take advantage of the many opportunities available in the city, such as museums, art, music, and parks. Getting to church on Sunday is a challenge, however. I have to want to get there. Traffic and parking present many obstacles. Street people with their requests for change are frequent greeters outside the church building. When I finally arrive inside the doors, I am always glad to be there. The effort to get there is great, but always worth it.

The communion set made of pottery by a friend of mine from high school is always present on the communion table, a visible reminder, like the baptismal font, of the sacraments we affirm. On the table in the rear of the sanctuary is a large plastic water bottle. Funds to support our lunch program for homeless people had been drastically reduced, so our church decided to see if we could voluntarily increase our congregational commitment to this food program. We are asked to put a quarter into the bottle for each time we eat a meal out at a restaurant during the week.

Guests from the overnight shelter may join us for worship or for coffee hour after worship. Announcements in the bulletin remind us of the need for volunteers to work at the community shelter we sponsor with other neighborhood congregations from November through March of each year. The Minute for Mission asks us to consider joining with another church member to prepare and serve a Sunday evening meal once a quarter at a house for persons who are living with AIDS.

The people with whom Jesus ate, the children he welcomed in God's name, those who came to him for healing, and his own parables about guests at banquet feasts become more than just remembered characters or stories. Getting to church and worshiping there have become for me a rehearsal of the world that God intends.

As our congregation comes forward at the end of the service to bring our offerings, we join in a circle around the communion table for our time of prayers of joy and thanksgiving, prayers for the world, and prayers for particular people. Everyone is invited to offer their spoken and silent prayers. Visitors introduce themselves, and we are blessed and sing our response to the benediction. We then leave to go to fellowship at coffee hour.

I choose to be a part of this worshiping congregation because it challenges my faith and expects me to go forth into the world from the table at which I am fed, at which I pray, at which I am welcomed. I am sent forth from this table each week, blessed for my faith journey and challenged to help bring into possibility the world as God intends it to be.

Liturgical and Educational Models

As in the previous chapters, here you will find suggestions for educational designs to use with groups in your congregation.

1. "Telling the Stories and Singing the Songs": An Intergenerational Study

These sessions are appropriate for church school, vacation church school, or a church family camp. They would also work well during summer church school, when connections among sessions are harder to make because participants may be sporadic in their attendance.

A complete model is provided for one session. Suggestions are given for biblical stories to use in additional sessions, which could follow the same design. The series is appropriate for participants from preschool (age three) to adults in age. If some adults are unfamiliar with intergenerational learning, it is important to help them understand their role, which is to work with a child or youth as a partner in the learning activities.

The model that follows uses a biblical story for the content. A song or hymn could be used in the same way. For example, you could teach a hymn, such as "Beautiful Jesus." If a person in the congregation knows sign language, everyone could learn to sign the hymn. Teach all the verses, then invite everyone to participate in learning centers in response to the hymn. To help remember the hymn, words to the verses could be printed on large pieces of paper and posted on the wall or on an easel. For nonreaders, the hymn could be recorded on a cassette tape and played.

Purpose. The purpose of these sessions is to hear and respond to biblical stories from the Old and New Testaments through music, art, and drama.

Objectives. By the end of these sessions, participants will have had a chance to do the following:

• Hear and discuss a biblical story.
• Sing a song that relates to the story.
• Respond to the story through art, music, or drama.

Room Setup. Have blank name tags available for people as they arrive. Think of having name tags in the shape of a symbol related to the biblical story being taught. Have water-based markers and tape available for people to use.

You will need a room large enough for everyone to sit together in the middle, with tables (child and adult sized) arranged around the walls of the room for the learning centers. Have quilts on the floor for those who would like to sit there, and chairs placed behind the quilts in a semicircle. Place a chair in the middle for the storyteller.

Resources. Find someone in the congregation who is a good storyteller to tell the biblical story. It is important that the person *tell* the story, not just read it. A good resource for biblical stories is the book *Young Children and Worship* by Jerome W. Berryman and Sonja M. Stewart (Louisville: Westminster/John Knox, 1989). If you plan to continue this class for several sessions, you could find several teenagers or adults to use as storytellers. Plan to meet with them so they can practice telling their story. Remind them that props are very helpful.

As you choose which biblical stories to use, look at the lectionary passages for the Sundays you are offering the class. See if one of those passages can be used. The United Church of Christ's church school curriculum, *The Inviting Word,* offers excellent background information on the lectionary passages. Look especially at the leader's guide for any of the age groups. An additional resource included with this curriculum is *Imaging the Word,* which has art, poetry, and writings appropriate for use with the lectionary readings.

Other sources of help in telling biblical stories from the lectionary are the curriculum of the United Church of Canada, *The Whole People of God,* and Carolyn C. Brown's books on planning for children in worship, *Forbid Them Not: Involving Children in Sunday Worship,* Years A, B, and C (Nashville: Abingdon Press, 1994).

Activities. Each session should include the following activities:

1. *Beginning the session* (10–15 minutes): Begin by welcoming everyone and singing a hymn together. Then invite the storyteller to come forward and tell the story to the group. As an example, we will use Jesus parable of the sower (Matt. 13:1–9). Appropriate hymns would be "Beautiful Jesus" and "For the Beauty of the Earth."

After the story, describe the learning centers and invite everyone to find a partner at least ten years older to work with at a center.

2. *Developing the session* (35 minutes): Have tables set up with needed materials so the learners can respond to the story. It is important to have a person at each center to help explain what the learners are to do. Remember that older children and youth can help to do this as well as adults.

You can set up the following learning centers or think of some of your own:

- Art Center. Have construction paper, crayons, markers, scissors, and glue available for those who would like to illustrate the story.
- Nature Center. Have available small plastic pots or cups, dirt, some pebbles (to put in the bottom of a pot or cup for drainage), some seeds (for marigolds or herbs), and a watering can. This center involves learners in planting seeds like those described in the parable.
- Drama Center. Some learners might be interested in acting out the story. The storyteller could be involved here in retelling the story and helping learners to dramatize the different kinds of seeds, soil, and rocks.
- Sowing Seeds in Good Soil. Have a long sheet of paper on the wall to make a mural. You can begin with a blank mural, or you

could draw the different parts of the story in advance. Invite learners to respond with their own drawings or with pictures or articles from magazines to illustrate seeds sown on the path, seeds sown in rocky soil, seeds planted among thorns, and seeds planted in good soil. Some learners might enjoy illustrating their answer to this question: If we are like God's seeds planted in good soil, what should we be doing in this world?

• Music Center. A song about this parable, called "The Sower," has been written and recorded by the Medical Mission Sisters on the album *Knock, Knock* (available from Avant Guard Records, 250 W. 57th Street, New York, N.Y. 10019). Participants in this center could listen to the song and begin to learn it.

3. *Concluding the session* (10 minutes): Gather everyone together to share anything they have done or made. If there are learners who participated in the drama center, they could act out the parable for the group.

Conclude with a prayer.

2. "Table Connections": A Program Linking Table Fellowship at Home and Church

This intergenerational design includes four sessions appropriate for children (three years and older), youth, and adults. The sessions can stand alone, or they can be taught as a unit. They can be used in a church school setting or during a church family meal. The sessions are also useful during times of teaching and learning about the communion; they are particularly appropriate on World Communion Sunday, Maundy Thursday, or even Thanksgiving, Christmas, and Easter. The season of stewardship education is also an appropriate time for thinking about the table we share.

Suggestions are given for the title and purpose of each session. A limited number of teaching and learning activities are also suggested. The rest of the planning is left to you so that you can adapt the sessions to your particular congregational setting. If you decide to use some of these sessions, consider involving an intergenerational group of older children, youth, and adults in the planning and development.

Purpose. The purpose of these sessions is to reflect on the meals we share as families at home and as families of faith at church. These sessions can also help learners of all ages to remember biblical stories of the meals Jesus shared and to make connections between those meals and the meals we eat today.

Objectives. By the end of the sessions, learners will have had the chance to:

- share stories about table meals at home.
- recall biblical stories of Jesus sharing meals.
- name some meanings for communion, the meal we share at church.
- identify ways our meals at home and church can include others, even strangers.

Session One: "Our Family Table"

Purpose. The purpose of this session is to share stories of family meals around the table at home.

Session Two: "Meals Jesus Shared"

Purpose. The purpose of this session is to tell and illustrate stories about the people with whom Jesus shared a meal.

Session Three: "The Table at Church"

Purpose. The purpose of this session is to discuss the meaning and purpose of communion.

Session Four: "Sharing from Our Table"

Purpose. The purpose of this session is to identify ways that the bounty from our tables at home and at church can be shared in the community with those who do not have food to eat or a table at which to eat it.

Activities. From the list of activities that follows, choose those that are most appropriate to your setting:

1. Draw pictures and tell stories about family meals shared on a daily basis and on special occasions.
2. Tell, discuss, and illustrate stories from the Gospels about Jesus eating with others.

3. Read and discuss Acts 2:37–47. How is your church like the early church described in Acts? How is it different?
4. Discuss the meanings of Holy Communion. Make place mats for home using the symbols of the meal.
5. Have a hands-on project related to helping provide food for those who don't have any. Consider packing food boxes for the homeless. Work to clean and organize the food pantry for the homeless if there is one at your church.
6. Brainstorm ways to share tables at home with those who live alone or in nursing homes.

3. "Habits of Discipleship": Finding a Rhythm of Spirituality

Included here are four sessions for adults of all ages. You could also offer these sessions to older youth and adults. Often, older adolescents enjoy opportunities to converse with adults other than their parents.

I have suggested a title and a purpose for each session, followed by a list of possible activities. These activities can be matched with appropriate sessions according to the needs of the learners. The model is purposely left open-ended so that you can adapt it to the needs of your congregation.

The sessions can be used in a church school setting, as an evening class during vacation church school, as the topic for a retreat, or once a week during the season of Lent. (Some of the sessions could be expanded so that the series would last for six weeks during Lent.) These sessions also work well in a retirement center or nursing home. Consider teaching them with a mixture of people from your congregation and another location, such as a house where developmentally delayed adults live or a house for persons who are living with AIDS.

Purpose. Just as rising, eating, working, and going to bed are rhythms in our lives, nurturing our lives of faith can also become a natural and daily rhythm. Many people find that habits of reading, meditation, prayer, and silence help them focus and find a sense of peace. The purpose of these sessions is to help adults explore ways to form such habits.

Meeting across the ages is helpful because people can share where they struggle with spiritual discipline as well as what they have found to be meaningful and important in their faith journey. It is essential that adults make nurturing their own faith a priority, so that they can then keep their baptismal promises to share their faith and nurture the faith of others.

Objectives. By the end of the sessions, learners will have had the opportunity to do the following:

- Identify the variety of ways they can be involved in some form of spiritual discipline.
- Share experiences of a life of spiritual devotion (and especially the techniques individuals have found that work for them).
- Identify a personal need and a commitment.
- Become familiar with helpful resources for nurturing a spiritual life.

Room Setup. The setup for the room depends on the activities being used in a particular session. Try to use the space and seating arrangements that will be most helpful in enabling conversation.

Session One: "The Spiritual Rhythm of My Life"
Purpose. The purpose of this session is to help participants discover and examine their current spiritual formation activities.

Session Two: "Spiritual Habits for a Life of Faith"
Purpose. The purpose of this session is to become familiar with a variety of ways of developing habits of spirituality.

Session Three: "Resources for Prayer and Meditation"
Purpose. The purpose of this session is to become familiar with resources useful in developing habits of discipleship.

Session Four: "Habits of Discipleship"
Purpose. The purpose of this session is to identify and discuss commitments to a spiritual rhythm, techniques the learners would like to try.

Activities. From the following list of activities, choose those that best fit your setting:

1. View and discuss the video *Discovering Everyday Spirituality,* hosted by Thomas Moore. (Available from Ecufilm, 1-800-251-4091.)

2. View and discuss the video *Praying in the Midst of Life.* There are six segments in the series, about twenty minutes each. Those that are particularly applicable to this topic include "Our Questions about Prayer," "Finding God," "Praying the Scripture," "Learning the Breath Prayer," and "Retreating at Any Time." (Available from Ecufilm, 1-800-251-4091.)

3. View and discuss the segment "What Good Is Prayer?" from the video series *Questions of Faith.* (Available from Ecufilm, 1-800-251-4091.)

4. Read and discuss selections from Kathleen Norris's *Dakota: A Spiritual Geography* (New York: Ticknor and Fields, 1993). Ecufilm also has a video featuring Kathleen Norris in their *Faces on Faith* series. *Dakota* is a book about space, a life of faith, and one woman's search for spirituality.

5. Read, discuss, and practice the different forms of prayer described in Richard Foster's *Prayer: Finding the Heart's True Home* (San Francisco: Harper San Francisco, 1992).

6. Invite your minister to come and share her or his habits of spiritual formation.

7. Read and discuss what others have written about practices of personal spiritual formation. Look at books by Henri Nouwen, Thomas Merton, Dorothy Day, and Madeleine L'Engle.

8. Have available a variety of devotional books for examination by the learners. Include *Weavings: A Journal of the Christian Spiritual Life* and *Alive Now!* (both published by Upper Room in Nashville). *These Days* is a devotional resource available from the Presbyterian Church (U.S.A.). Two new resources are available from the United Church Press: *In Good Company* is a journal for spiritual reflection designed for women, and *The Book of Daily Prayer* is a devotional book based on the daily lectionary readings. The latter includes scripture, reflections on the scripture, and prayers.

After learners have had time to look over these resources, provide an opportunity for everyone to comment on what they examined and how useful they think it would be for them.

9. Plan one session that allows learners to experience a time of meditation and prayer. Have comfortable chairs available, and create an environment that invites reflection. Set up a worship center in the room with objects that have meaning for you. When I have set up such a center, I have placed a cloth or table runner on the table, a candle, a plant or vase of flowers, an open Bible, and any other appropriate symbols.

Use this session to model what is possible. Begin with a time of focusing and quiet. Then invite people to reflect on scripture that you read; try reading a psalm. Provide paper and pens, and after the reading, invite learners to silently reflect on the scripture, either in prayer or in writing. Then invite participants to share their responses. Conclude with a prayer.

After a few minutes of quiet, invite the learners to discuss the meditative process. What parts of the process had most meaning for them? Which of the activities are already a part of their personal spiritual discipline? Which would they like to include?

10. Look at a denominational resource on daily prayer. What elements are involved? Which parts are most usable in a life of prayer and devotion?

11. Engage in a study of nine different biblical forms of prayer by using the study book *Prayers of the Bible for a Faithful Journey,* by Elizabeth F. Caldwell and Earle Hilgert. (Available from Horizons, 1-800-487-4875.) Included with this study book is a leader's guide with suggestions for teaching the nine forms.

12. Discuss the meaning of the terms *prayer, spiritual formation, meditation, devotion,* and *habits of discipleship.*

13. Identify and discuss practices and disciplines for spiritual formation in light of your own and your participants experiences. Touch on the following practices: worshiping God together; telling the Christian story to one another; interpreting the Scriptures and finding meanings in them for personal lives of faith; praying, confessing our sins, forgiving, and being reconciled to others; encouraging others in their lives of faith and vocation; carrying out specific faithful acts of service and witness; being neighbors to one another; providing hospitality and care to others, especially strangers; struggling to understand the nature and demands of the communities in which we live; working against powers of evil in the world, which work to destroy God's creation; and working together to maintain structures that sustain God's creation.

(These practices are taken from "Growing in the Life of the Christian Faith," a study document of the Presbyterian Church [U.S.A.].)

14. In his book *Prayer: Finding the Heart's True Home,* Richard J. Foster says, "We today yearn for prayer and hide from prayer. We are attracted to it and repelled by it. We believe prayer is something we should do, even something we want to do, but it seems like a chasm stands between us and actually praying. We experience the agony of prayerlessness."[16] Ask participants to respond to this statement.

15. Read and discuss the findings of the Search Institute study "Effective Christian Education." A summary of the findings can be found in the book *The Teaching Church* by Eugene C. Roehlkepartain (Nashville: Abingdon Press, 1993). (The study itself is available from the Search Institute, 1-800-888-7828.)

Of particular interest is the finding that a majority of adult church members do not pray or read the Bible. The study also found that parents want their children to have a lifelong faith, yet "two-thirds of families rarely or never have family devotions; more than half the teenagers don't talk to their father about faith or God. A third don't talk to their mothers. Two-thirds of families don't do family projects to help others."[17] Ask participants to assess how the adults in your congregation would respond if posed with the same questions asked in the study.

Eating in Order to See Better

A Call to Commitment

Come!
Let us celebrate the supper of our Lord,
Let us all together
Bake a giant loaf
And together prepare the jars of wine
As at the wedding feast in Cana.

Let the women not forget the salt
Nor the men the leaven.
And let us invite many guests:
The lame, the blind, the deaf,
The poor.

Quickly now!
Let us follow the recipe of our Lord,
Let us together knead the dough with our hands
And watch with joy
The rising Bread.

Because today we are celebrating
Our commitment to Christ Jesus.
Today we are renewing our commitment
To the kingdom,
and no one shall go hungry away.[18]

This poem by Elsa Támez serves as a reminder of the meaning of communion, both the sacrament itself and that which we take with us as we move out from the table. "The recipe" that she describes is like the living bread that Jesus spoke of. The bread and the cup we share at the table go with us into the world as living reminders of that which we affirm, that which we celebrate, and that to which we are called to remember by our baptism.

Two recent occurrences have deepened our understanding of the sacrament of communion. First, the communion liturgy has changed. New forms of the Great Prayer of Thanksgiving and the responses spoken and sung by the congregation, a wealth of new communion hymns, and a variety of new forms of communing have enriched our knowledge of and participation in the sacrament.

Second, the celebration has become much more open and frequent. Like many other adults, I was denied a place at the table until my confirmation indicated that I had "joined" the church. Then and only then was I welcomed to the table, five times a year: the first Sunday of each quarter and Christmas Eve.

Now we welcome baptized children to Christ's Table. Communion is served once a month in many congregations, and every Sunday in others. The changes in who is welcome and how often the meal is served are visible reminders of the transforming power of the sacrament.

The rhythm of the meal at Christ's Table serves to keep us in balance, to connect us literally to God's food. We eat food at our family tables in order to be nourished, to grow, to be strong. We eat food at the table where Jesus Christ is the host in order to see better, says Rubem Alves:

> People know that it is the Spirit's doing by the new things that begin to happen. The eyes change, and the heart as well. It is because the heart is different that the eyes begin to see things that one had not seen before. . . . It is the words [of the liturgy] that make the difference. Jesus did not give only the bread and the wine; eating was not enough. It was necessary to see with new eyes. To eat in order to see better. He mixed the words of love and promises in the food, to cure our blindness.[19]

We come to Christ's Table expecting new things to happen, hoping to see the world differently, with new hopes and visions. We come because we need the words of God and the food of God to move us from the table into the world, where God calls us to be.

6 A Sacramental Model of Education in the Church

In her book *Fashion Me a People: Curriculum in the Church,* Maria Harris introduces an artistic model of educational planning. The components of this model are not unlike those of Thomas Groome's shared praxis model.[1] Both models are praxis based. They require discussion, analysis, reflection on present practice, and commitment to new action in light of our calling as faithful Christians.

This concluding chapter offers a sacramental model of education based on Harris's artistic model. It can be used with a church committee or group interested in thinking about how such a model of education could be implemented in their setting. Each step of the model will be explained along the way. The model can be used step-by-step over a series of months. It can also serve as the design for a planning retreat of committees or officers. It might also be the topic of an adult church school class.

1. Contemplation—Considering the Whole Design

In thinking about a sacramental model of education, the image that comes to mind for me is that of a quilt. I have always been fascinated with quilts: the process of making them, what they reveal about the maker, and the stories they tell.

In a book about quilts and their history, Roderick Kiracofe says that "quilts, like diaries, are an accumulation of bits and pieces of the maker's life, a repository of ideas, hopes, and feelings."[2] He continues: "Beyond their aesthetic value, however, quilts exist as a form of personal expression. They recall a brave, genuine, creative spirit. Those women who signed, initialed, or dated their work in thread left traces of themselves on the fabric. They might add an embroidered or inked inscription, often highly sentimental rhymes or moral precept, to express something of their intentions to us across the years. . . . Quilting was and continues to be women's way of making a valuable social contribution through their own handiwork."[3]

The author wonders if the careful and meticulous process of quilt making provided a way for women "to express themselves on deeper, more creative levels." He concludes: "Just as quilting parties brightened a pioneer woman's social circle, the quilts themselves—sometimes even mere swatches of cloth tucked into a letter—became talismans of old friends and loved ones who were far away."[4]

Notice the themes that emerge from these observations about quilts and their makers:

- Quilts reveal something about the maker. They are, in a real sense, a personal expression.
- The process of making a quilt is connectional. Quilting parties are a communal commitment to creating something. Quilt squares, lovingly designed and stitched, connect the maker to a friend or loved one far away.
- The entire process of quilt making is a creative expression. Though quilting patterns have been passed down through networks of families and friends, each quilt is unique because of the person or group involved in making it. Each person who works on a quilt provides her or his own way of stitching. Like fingerprints, the stitches of no two people are identical.
- The quilt serves a purpose, both practical and social. Quilts are used for warmth. They also provide opportunities for people to share the products of their handiwork with each other, their families, and friends.
- The finished quilt tells a story. The choices of patterns and stitching all contribute to the intentions of the maker.

Programs and Quilts

Often, congregations are focused on maintaining current programs of religious education. I remember working with a Christian Education

Committee as its members met to plan their work for the year. They proceeded to list everything they were responsible for and assumed that if all of the items were addressed at some time during the year, they would have accomplished their assignment. I remember asking them about what wasn't being done. What dreams did they have, what visions for new commitments in the area of Christian education?

I also remember working with a Worship Committee. When I met with the person chairing the committee, I suggested beginning each meeting with an educational moment. This could be a time for the committee to learn about worship—liturgy, music, the arts, the seasons of the church year. In my mind, I had planned a year's worth of moments for educating about worship. The chair of the committee looked at me and said the committee wasn't really necessary, since it was the minister's job to lead worship.

Models of religious education and patterns of worship are vital parts of the life of a household of faith. Left unexamined, they can become maintenance oriented rather than life forming. When the worship life and the educational life of a congregation are understood as separate entities, members of the congregation cannot see and make connections between what they learn, why they worship, and how they live a life of faith.

Just as quilts reveal something about the maker, so do educational programs and worship speak about a congregation's priorities. The process of making a quilt is creative. It invites personal expression, just like the educational programs of a congregation bear the unique marks of their planners, teachers, and leaders.

When a quilt is completed, the symbols used in the pattern tell a story. Each part of the needlework communicates something about the one who stitched the quilt. So too, households of faith tell stories about their commitments to living the Christian faith. These stories are revealed in the ways they worship, educate, and pass on the faith.

Questions for Reflection

1. Think about your congregation, your household of faith. What do you believe to be the priorities of this household? How are resources (people, time, and money) allocated? Think of your congrega-

tion in terms of a quilt. If the squares on the quilt represent the priorities of the congregation, what symbols would you use to represent these priorities?

2. What is the relationship between the educational life and the worship life of your congregation?

3. What evidence do you see of the creative expression of the people in your congregation?

4. In what ways are parents and families supported in intentional ways of living the Christian faith in their daily lives?

5. If you had to state the purpose of your congregation's approach to religious education, what would you say?

6. Reflect on the worship life of your congregation. For whom is it planned? Who is welcomed into worship?

7. What education about the sacraments takes place in your household of faith? What connections are made between including the sacraments in worship and living out the sacraments in daily life?

2. Engagement—Stepping Back to See More Clearly

One of my nephews has a much loved quilt made for him by his grandmother. It was a gift to him when he was born. Over the years it has become thinner, grayer, and more frayed. He was looking at it recently and asked me if new eyelet fringe could be added to the borders of the blanket. I told him it would be hard to do, since the material was so thin and worn. Adding new material might tear it. The only thing I knew that could be done would be to make a cover for the blanket. He didn't think that was such a great idea, since then his blanket wouldn't be the same at all. He was right!

Occasionally when he is examining his quilt very closely, he will ask me to tell him the story of how he got the quilt. It's a story he's heard many times, but one he never tires of. I think he likes to have me tell the story because it is personal and reminds him of who he is in the family. His quilt is a comfort to him. Now that he is older, it stays at home, waiting for him at bedtime. When turning off the light to sleep, I often hear him ask, "Turn the light back on, please, I need to find Dee Dee's face." He turns the corners of the quilt until he comes to the most familiar one, her face. The location of the face is known only to him.

The second part of our model, engagement, is a time of stepping back in order to see more clearly, to get a larger picture of what is going on within the household of faith. This step requires critical thinking abilities and honest assessment. It is essential to focus on the following questions:

- What do we want to continue doing as a congregation?
- What is no longer appropriate? In other words, what do we need to let go of?
- What is missing? What are we failing to do that is needed at this time in the life of the congregation?

For an example of this kind of assessment, let's take a look at vacation church school. Many churches have a long tradition of offering daily vacation church school for children during one week of the summer. Educationally, it is wonderful to have the chance to plan intensive teaching and learning sessions for a one-week period. Denominational publishers each year make available creative and easy-to-use curricula designed for children at the preschool, elementary, and junior high levels.

Several unexamined assumptions continue to dominate this program of religious education, however. For instance, most vacation church school curricula assume the following: a daily morning schedule of classes; age-graded groups; adults willing to direct the program; trained adult teachers; space for outdoor as well as indoor groups to meet and play; money to buy workbooks for children; leader's guides for adults; and resources for teaching and learning.

Issues that don't seem to be addressed in such curricula include congregations with small numbers of children; congregations with few adults available for teaching during the day; churches in urban settings with little space or money available for the program; intergenerational groups; and adults who would like to participate in a summer learning experience.

One congregation knew that a vacation church school experience for children during the day would not work because so many of the parents worked outside the home and were not available to send their children. They planned a week-long evening experience, Sunday through Thursday nights. It began with a meal, and then people were divided by age groups.

The program worked well for the adult groups; their classes were well conceived and planned. The children and youth classes, however, were not. No curricula or activities were made available to the teachers. Each was left to make his or her own decisions about what was going to be taught.

What was missing was intentional planning for all age groups. The child and youth classes lacked the thoughtful planning processes in place for the adult groups.

There are parts of my nephew's quilt that can be mended, places where new pieces of material can be added or patched. There are, however, those places that cannot be changed. This is also true of congregations as they engage in the task of critically assessing their education and worship.

Questions for Reflection

1. What in your congregation's program of education do you want to affirm and continue doing? What in the worship life of this household of faith is valuable and nurturing?

2. What in religious education and worship is no longer appropriate and needs to be let go of?

3. What issue, group, or need is not being addressed? Does your congregation make a place for young adults to be a part of the life, work, and worship of the church? What about the welcome to single parents? What religious education opportunities are made available to children, youth, or adults with special needs, either physical or mental?

3. Form Giving—Creating the Pattern

The preceding chapters have articulated meanings and experiences of the sacraments and their relationship to our lives of faith. If congregations and families are going to live faithfully in response to the sacraments, there must be a commitment to a sacramental model of religious education. Such a model includes six conceptual frameworks: congregational affirmations, household commitments, pastoral priorities, table fellowship, sacramental blessings, and community hospitality. As your read over the descriptions of these concepts, consider the ways they are already at work in the life of your congregation.

Congregational Affirmations

The boy was sitting at a table in a restaurant after church. An adult passed by the table and noticed what he had on his head and complimented him on the American Indian headdress. The boy sat up very straight and told the adult, "This is not a headdress, these are flames of fire." It was Pentecost Sunday, and his church had celebrated this special day with a Pentecost party that included making flames of fire to wear.

His church is located in downtown Milwaukee, and it ensures the presence of all ages in the educational and worship life of the congregation. Children are included in the first part of worship and then leave to go to church school, which lasts for the rest of worship and for the hour after worship when adults are in class. On communion Sundays, children stay with their parents for worship.

At a recent meeting of the church's Worship Committee, the sacrament of baptism was being discussed. Working with the ministers, this committee had decided to designate four Sundays in the year when baptisms would take place: the Baptism of Jesus (in January), Easter, Pentecost, and Christian Education Sunday (in the fall). In selecting these particular Sundays, they were choosing to say to the congregation that baptisms were not just for the families of those being baptized, but for the whole congregation. Establishing baptisms on these particular Sundays enabled the ministers to plan worship around the sacrament so as to proclaim its meaning for everyone in worship.

At this particular meeting, they were discussing how baptisms took place early in the worship. Most books of worship, however, place the liturgy of baptism after the Word is read and proclaimed. In the middle of discussing the pros and cons of moving the sacrament to a later place in worship, one of the officers reminded the group that if they moved it, the children would not be there to participate. The issue was settled.

Children are important in the life of this congregation. Their minister, the Reverend Deborah Block, has intentionally worked with the Education Committee to design programs that meet the needs of the whole congregation. This thinking and planning has resulted in four annual intergenerational events. They take place during Lent, Advent, Pentecost and one other time of the liturgical year.

On Passion Sunday or Palm Sunday, all ages meet together after worship to reenact the events in the last week of the life of Jesus. A parade of people takes the learners into the fellowship room, where everyone is invited to wear a costume or a headpiece and to share in a meal like Jesus would have had with the disciples. Certain adults take on the role of disciples and tell stories about Jesus. The ministers then talk about the last meal that Jesus shared with his disciples before his death. The meanings of communion are explained, bread and juice is shared, and the doxology is sung. A small room is set up like the Gethsemane garden, and families are invited to share a family prayer and the Prayer of Jesus there.

One year, the first Sunday in Lent was celebrated by asking a potter to bring his potter's wheel. Learners of all ages were invited to imprint sacramental symbols of wheat, shells, and grapes onto a disk of clay the size of a coaster. The potter fired the disks, and everyone was invited to take home their sacramental symbol to keep as a reminder during Lent.

Each year the Pentecost Party celebrates the life of the church. Other important events take place at this party: the recognition of church school teachers, the ordination and installation of church officers, and the welcoming of youth confirmed into church membership. A highlight of this intergenerational event is a Pentecost cake. The candles on the cake are used to remind everyone of the children's baptisms.

The role of church school teachers is also emphasized in September when classes begin. Teachers are commissioned in worship. Questions of promise and support are first asked of parents, then the congregation. Last, the children are asked to stand and make their promises, and then they follow their teachers out to begin their learning together.

Each year, the congregation looks forward to preparing the Advent devotional booklet. Deborah selects a theme and invites children, youth, and adults to make a contribution to this worship resource used during the season of Advent.

The commitment of this congregation and its ministers to affirm the presence, participation, and leadership of children ensures that the youngest ones will grow up knowing they are valued members of this household of faith.[5]

A sacramental model of education is affirmed by a congregation when

- the presence of children in worship and education is intentionally considered and planned;
- opportunities to be a household of faith—with people of all ages learning and worshiping together—is a congregational value;
- those who teach and lead children are honored and supported;
- the developmental needs and abilities of people of all ages are thoughtfully considered in planning worship and education;
- parents are supported in their commitment to nurture their child's life of faith;
- pastors are committed to the inclusion of children in the life of the congregation.

Household Commitments

Every now and then, I have the pleasure of meeting a seminary student who possesses a spirituality that is remarkable. Renae is a single mother of two teenagers. When I first met her, I was impressed with her presence and the way she articulated her faith. I also sensed that she was a woman of great depth and that in my conversations with her I, the teacher, would become the learner.

My first impressions were correct. During a year when she experienced the death of one of her brothers and both of her parents, she moved through trying times with a faith that never waned. She wrote a poem, entitled "Being Renewed: The Face of My Faith":

> . . . My Feet May be Tired but My Soul
> Does Magnify the Lord
> And then, I Risssssse
> I Risssssssse
> Like Mother Olivia
> Who Pusssshed me Forth
> From her Waters
> and now I Pusssssh forth
> Wading in the Water
> Reaching, Clinging, Holding on to
> A Hope and A Prayer
> That One Day
> We Will All Re-Member
> Goddddddddd
> the Holy of Holies
> Who has Brought US thus Far
> On the Way
> And
> Be Re-Newed[6]

Renae grew up in a household of faith. Her father's strong verbal expressions of faith both spoken and sung were matched with the equally strong yet silent and implicit faith of her mother. In writing about this poem, which was inspired by the face of her mother's faith, Renae says, "I find myself re-turning to my ancestor's household of faith to be empowered and renewed by their amazing strength and determination."[7]

Renae's faith has been formed and continues to be nurtured in the commitments she makes to her own household of faith. In a corner of her living room she has created a worship space. In this space is a picture of Christ, carvings from Africa, photographs of family members who have died, a cup of fresh flowers, a map of Africa, books, ears of dried corn, pine cones, a Bible, a candle, and a tape of gospel music.

She says that this worship center keeps her centered. It reminds her of where she has come from and where she is going to go, people who have been faithful, who have given her instructions. The symbols change from time to time, but they always represent her journey of faith.

Renae has graduated from seminary. Her oldest son will graduate from high school in a year. Her younger son has said he will go wherever she wants to go. She is waiting to find out the place her ministry will call her to. She is sitting with a face of faith.

I believe that instinctively, Renae knows that one of the best ways to pass on faith to her children is to live a life of faith. Her children see her worship space, they watch her read her Bible and pray just as she watched her father and mother, and so the face of faith is passed on to another generation.

A sacramental model of education is marked by household commitments that

- affirm Christian family traditions;
- make room for individuals to express their faith, each in their own way;
- honor faces of faith and the variety of their expressions;
- provide room, resources, and time for reading, reflection, and prayer;
- encourage moments of contemplation;
- acknowledge the need of adults to take care of their faith so as to enable faith in children;
- recognize the balance between the doing of a life of faith in mission and witness and the being of faith in meditation, scripture reading, and prayer.

Pastoral Priorities

I have a friend who was hired part-time as a minister of education. One of the first things he did was to look at the place where church school classes met. He found a nice space, but it looked very uninviting. Being an educator, he knew the importance of an educational setting that said, "Something is going to happen here."

He also met teachers who were anxious to have someone help them plan for teaching in the church school, especially in regard to the curriculum they would use. Mark began to work with the teachers. He listened to their needs and concerns. They agreed that working on the classrooms was a priority, as was the curriculum.

It was not difficult to find people willing to help clean and decorate the rooms. Bright curtains were added to coordinate with the paint colors. Stencils were carefully painted as borders on the walls. Bright signs were painted by an artist in the congregation, identifying each age group in the church.

While church members worked on decorating the rooms, Mark was busy writing a curriculum for the teachers to use. He coordinated the curriculum with seasonal themes and lectionary readings that would be used in worship. As I spoke with Mark over the first few months of his working with this congregation, I could hear the enthusiasm in his voice. He was having a wonderful time working and planning with these people.

The minister of the church announced his resignation six months after Mark was hired. The congregation and Mark had really enjoyed working with each other, and Mark decided he wanted to apply for the position of minister. He did, and they unanimously voted to extend him a call. As I was walking through the building with him just prior to his installation, he proudly showed me the rooms they had decorated. He was also proud of the fact that he was continuing to write the curriculum for teachers to use with the children and youth in the church school. It was obvious that he loved finding ways to ensure that what was learned in church school was related to the worship service. He was committed to this effort because he wanted to integrate the two parts of Sunday morning—education and worship.[8]

I have never asked Mark to describe himself to me, but I think if I did he would probably put *teacher* at the top of the list. He is a minister for whom education is not something that you hire someone else to do because you don't have the time, interest, or ability. Religious education is at the core of Mark's understanding of who he is, called by God to be a minister of the Word and sacrament.

A sacramental model of education is truly possible in a congregation, but only if ministers can see the potential to integrate education and worship. Often, these two core activities of the church are separate in the minds of the congregation because they are separate in the minds of ministers. Ministers know they are expected to be responsible for the worshiping life of the congregation; being responsible for their educational life is not always a priority.

A sacramental model of education is marked by clear pastoral priorities and is evidenced in a congregation when a minister

- knows what curriculum is being used in the church school at every level, not just in the adult classes;
- visits every class during the church school year;
- works as part of a teaching team with other adults;
- has short-term teaching experience at every level of the church school over a three- to five-year period;
- makes reference in sermons to church school curriculum and activities;
- serves as a resource person to the Worship and Christian Education Committees as together they discuss and plan for the integration of their two responsibilities;
- shares stories about the church school in worship at times other than the beginning and end of the church school year;
- participates in or leads a continuing education event for church leaders;
- knows the first names of all the children and youth in the church;
- has had experience teaching youth prior to leading them in confirmation classes;
- is acquainted with denominational resource centers and encourages church members to use them;
- reads current literature in the fields of religious education, liturgy, worship, and the sacraments;
- has at least one children's book in her or his office;
- feels as comfortable talking with a three-year-old and a fourteen-year-old as with an adult.

Table Fellowship

It was spring, and time to honor graduating seniors in worship on Sunday. It was Nona's first year serving as an associate pastor on the staff of a large suburban congregation. She had been told it was a tradition to give a gift to the seniors. She knew that in the past they had been given key chains with the Presbyterian seal, pins, or books. She was looking for something different, something that might not get left behind when they packed to go away to college. She was searching for something that would carry meaning and be a symbol of the place of the church in their lives.

The day arrived, and each graduating senior came with their family to worship. It was a special time for the congregation to mark this transition in the life of its young people, a way of connecting the holy with the daily.

The time came for the giving of the gift to the seniors, and Nona rose for the presentation. The gift was both simple and symbolic; she had prepared a small loaf of bread for each young person. In giving them this loaf of bread, she wanted them to remember their congregation, a congregation where many of them had been baptized and confirmed. She wanted them to know that on the occasions of celebrating the sacrament of communion, when the bread was broken and the cup was shared, they would be remembered. The table fellowship of the congregation would go with them as a reminder of their place within the household of faith. And when they had vacations from school and they returned home, they would be welcomed home to table fellowship.

When Nona told me this story, I was struck by the powerful simplicity of this gift. I remembered dreading that time of the year when I would get calls from colleagues asking, "What gift can we give our graduating seniors? I can't think of a thing." Nona gave them bread, a simple reminder of the power of their formation and nourishment as Christians called to Christ's Table and called to move out from the table.[9]

A sacramental model of education is marked by table fellowship and is evidenced in a congregation when

- people are helped to make connections between Christ's Table and the tables they gather around every day;
- there are opportunities to learn and discuss the implications of the food from Christ's Table, the bread and the cup that have the power to feed us so we never hunger;
- children and their parents can learn about the meanings of the sacrament of communion;

- congregations make commitments to projects that involve sharing bread and other foods with those in need;
- strangers to the table are welcomed and are invited to family tables to share a meal;
- biblical stories of table fellowship are remembered and told to children.

Sacramental Blessings

When Tracy was hired as associate pastor for youth ministry, she knew the value of work-camp trips that involved youth and adults in mission projects. She planned the first trip and took sixteen youth and adults to West Virginia, where they repaired houses and a local community center. Seven years later she took fifty-six youth and thirteen adults to a site in Missouri, where they built a chapel for a camp for handicapped children and adults. The design for the chapel had been contributed by an architect in the congregation.

The program of youth ministry in her congregation involves youth in education (church school and confirmation), fellowship (youth groups), worship and mission (work camps). Each year, Tracy puts together a photo album of the work-camp trip from beginning to end. Planning for the next trip begins as soon as one ends. Stories and slides of the work-camp trip are shared by the youth in worship services after they return home.

Tracy and the other adults in the congregation who work with the youth are a sacramental blessing to them. These adults embody their baptismal promises and continue to feed these young people as they move from Christ's Table. In his book *Theological Themes in Youth Ministry,* William Myers uses the concept of *guarantors* to describe the kind of adults who should work with young people. Guarantors are adults who are both at home in and yet challenged by their faith. They are adults who are at a place in their life when they can guarantee for youth that adulthood is an okay place to be.

Tracy works with a church member who is a guarantor, Donna. Together they plan and lead the church's program of confirmation education. They have worked together on this program for years. A few years ago they decided to address the Christian Education Committee and the church officers about a problem that concerned them. The numbers participating in the yearlong confirmation program were growing so large that two groups were needed. That was the good news.

The bad news was that they had never seen or met many of the youth who showed up for confirmation. Many of these young people had been baptized in the congregation but had never been brought back for religious education. Some of them resented being made to attend confirmation education. When the time came to talk about the faith statement they would be expected to write and the date of their confirmation, some told Tracy and Donna that they did not want to be confirmed. Some simply refused. Others said, "I don't want to do this, but my parents are making me, so I'll do what they want—but it's not what I want."

Tracy and Donna struggled with the reality of such responses. They were concerned with the large gaps they saw between the baptismal blessing and the participation in the life of a household of faith. The blessing with water seemed incomplete in the lives of some of these youth because it had not been encouraged to grow—it had not been nurtured by participation in the life and worship of the congregation. Tracy and Donna were concerned that the church was confirming some youth right out the door of the church. The issue of individual choice to make or refuse to make a public affirmation of faith was also on their minds.

After a year of thought and struggle, they decided to work on a proposal to the governing board of the congregation. The proposal included a choice of two ways to mark the end to the confirmation process. The proposal was presented, approved, and implemented the following year.

The choice was left up to the youth themselves. On the Sunday when confirmation education ended, some youth chose to be recognized for the completion of the year of study. Another group of youth decided they were ready to make their public profession of faith and to be received as members of the congregation. This affirmation was made at a different service of worship. The youth who did not choose to make a public profession of faith were told that if they did decide to be confirmed, they could talk with the committee responsible for membership and then complete the process.

Tracy and Donna, of course, want all of the young people to complete the confirmation process by making a public profession of faith, but they know the reality of the youth they serve. They teach in the hope that those youth whose only experience of church since their baptism has been the confirmation class will find their way back to the congregation. They teach these baptized children of God, confident that God's Spirit is working in and through them as a sacramental blessing.[10]

A sacramental model of education is marked by sacramental blessing and is evidenced in a congregation when

- families follow through on their promise to raise their children in the Christian faith;
- families make participation in the household of faith a priority in their lives;
- members of the congregation intentionally find ways to live out the promises they make at a baptism, to help nurture children in the Christian faith;
- adults are willing to work with youth as guarantors;
- there is education about the sacraments and their meaning in the liturgy of worship and in daily life.

Community Hospitality

It is a large, urban, and wealthy congregation with a diverse staff of ministers. The education programs offered by the congregation are carefully and artistically described in printed brochures made available every quarter of the year. There is a group or class available for every age group in the church. The beautiful sanctuary, outstanding music program, and formal worship attract many visitors and new members every year.

Behind the obvious wealth and size of this church is a strong commitment to ministry with the surrounding neighborhood—with homeless persons and those living just off the streets in overpopulated and poorly maintained public housing. A social service center, a center for aging, and a counseling center are all vital programs of this congregation.

Equally important to this congregation is its ministry with children in the urban neighborhood surrounding the church buildings. John was hired as an associate pastor responsible for the mission programs of the congregation. He affirms that this church spends a great deal of time thinking about children, who are a focus of mission.

Visiting the families in public housing is one of John's priorities. He meets the families of those children who come to the after-school tutoring program at the church. In the program, one adult volunteer is matched with one child, and they work together during the school year.

The church used to have a problem with too many kids and not enough tutors. Then they came up with a marketing strategy. Children in the program make Christmas cards each year. The paper and printing are donated, and the church and local bookstores sell the cards. A local newspaper columnist always runs an article about the tutoring program and the cards. Now, the church sometimes has too many volunteers and so is faced with the "problem" of sharing volunteers with other church programs in the city.

Tutors in the program are a mixture of members and nonmembers, often young adults looking for an activity to provide some meaning in their lives. Several adults have worked with the same child for all six years of grammar school. The relationships built over the time of tutoring become important to both the child and the adult.

Two years ago, the church established the Center for Whole Life in a vacant apartment of a nearby housing project. Short-time child care is available for mothers who drop in for conversation, support, and nurture. Worship, prayer, and Bible study are also available for the women, who are mostly single mothers. This project was designed in direct response to the growth of the tutoring program. Believing that the way to really help children is to work with the parents and to get to children as early in their development as possible, the church ventured into the home environment.

Realizing that summer break from school does not always help children in urban settings, the church offers a summer day school for one hundred children over a five-week period. Public school teachers are hired to provide instruction as well as art experiences and recreation.

A scholarship program established by the church pays for a number of children to go to high school and college.

There is the potential for large, wealthy, and socially prominent churches to turn inward, ministering only to those inside the church. This congregation struggles with the reality of an urban setting, seeking ways to faithfully respond to God's call. They are reminded of this call in sermons, in classes, in worship—every time they approach the doors of the church and are first greeted by the outstretched hand of a homeless person looking for spare change.

This congregation's programs of social ministry are shared as a priority by all members. They are encouraged to find ways to live out their faith and share their time and talents in the community. Six or eight people gather each Sunday evening to cook a meal for the homeless. Families are encouraged to volunteer to cook together. At five-thirty, homeless people are invited in to share the meal with church members. Food cooked by the volunteers is shared with other shelters in the neighborhood.

I attended John's installation as associate pastor. The congregation was in the middle of a renovation and building program. Pews had been removed from the sanctuary, scaffolding and large plastic tarps framed the front of the worship area. The organ was being restored, and dust was everywhere. I thought it was a most appropriate setting for the installation of a minister responsible for mission. Being in mission is not always nice and neat. It gets messy sometimes. [11]

Being in a household of faith where community hospitality is a priority means you are willing to live with a challenging faith, a faith that disturbs an ordered and quiet lifestyle. This congregation attempts to faithfully live in response to the African proverb mentioned in an earlier chapter, "It takes a village to raise a child."

A sacramental model of education is marked by community hospitality and is evidenced in a congregation when

- the congregation's community and its needs are seriously addressed;
- people of all ages in the household of faith are involved in mission projects;
- programs of religious education enable people to make connections between the biblical story and faithful Christian living;

• education and worship work together to maintain the church's commitment to justice and wholeness of life for all of God's children.

4. Emergence—The Shape of the Model

The first two steps in this planning model provided you with a chance to reflect on and critique the educational and liturgical models at work in your congregation. The third step, form giving, described some visible marks of a sacramental model of education. In this fourth step, your awareness and analysis of the present situation is confronted by the possibilities of something new.

Chapters 2–5 have presented educational and liturgical models illustrative of a sacramental model of education. Consider the following questions:

• Which of these models are already being used in your congregation?
• Which models described in these chapters represent new ways of thinking for your congregation?
• What new ideas for integrating education and worship have emerged from your reading and discussion?
• If you had to make a list of priorities for the next year, where would you begin? What will it take to make these priorities a reality?
• What can your congregation affirm about the relationship between worship and education, between the holiness of the sacraments and the everydayness of living in the world?
• Some denominations have written descriptions of what they expect from church members. What would happen if your congregation made available a list of suggested household commitments —the ways that households could make explicit their partnership with the church in living faithful Christian lives? What would that list look like?
• What potential is there for sharing table fellowship and education programs with other congregations in the neighborhood?
• In what ways are opportunities for mission involvement made available to all persons in the church? What new mission opportunities can be added?

5. Release—Celebrating the Process and the Form

Recall the discussion of quilts at the beginning of this chapter. Consider the plans that have emerged from your thinking and creative dreaming. In what ways do these plans work to connect education and worship within the household of faith, both in the congregation and in the homes of church members?

What purpose do these plans serve? In what ways do these plans represent a connectional process? What creative expressions are encouraged? If a stranger came to this church, what stories would she or he hear?

Through the use of symbols, quilts tell a story—of love, friendship, the yearning for freedom, of hope and dreams and home. If you could create a symbol for a sacramental model of education, what would it be?

Come Unto Me

The religious leaders and the disciples were continually surprised by the people Jesus welcomed to his side and into his arms, and by the homes he was willing to enter. His invitation to "come unto me" was extended to a bent-over woman, to a much despised tax collector, to children of all ages, to women who grieved over the death of their brother, to parents who had lost a child.

Jesus broke the rules regarding who was acceptable to God. He consistently taught by his actions that the people who were welcome in God's realm were children, the poor, the sick, the lonely, those in need of a friend and a healing touch. When crowds gathered and parents pressed forward with their children for Jesus to bless, the disciples of Jesus tried to send them away. Didn't he have better things to do than to hold children on his lap and talk with them?

No, he did not. Time and time again he reminded his followers that to welcome a child was to welcome him. He told them to be attentive to children, because to look at children was to know what God's realm is like.

This book has tried through stories and models to rethink sacramental education in light of Jesus' invitation to "come unto me." Reflect again on Letty Russell's tools for rebuilding the household, discussed in the first chapter. She says we must do three things: practice hospitality, listen to the underside, and work to imagine what might be.

In what ways are these criteria being addressed in your congregation and in the homes of church members? How is hospitality expressed to all persons, whatever their age, shape, or place in life? Are children welcomed and encouraged to participate and lead?

How are the needs of the underside being met in your congregation and in your community? Who are the people of the underside? Who listens to them? Who invites them to participate in the life and work of the congregation?

What new programs, worship, and ways of living in response to the sacraments are yet to be imagined in the life of the congregation and its members? What new thinking needs to take place about the sacraments so as to live into God's realm?

People sought out Jesus for many reasons. The stories in the Gospels remind us that for many, just being with Jesus was enough. The invitation he graciously extended to everyone he met was one of sacramental presence. His face of faith reminded people of who they were and who they were called to be as children of God.

Every time we participate in a baptism, as we watch the water gently washing a child's face, we remember that the waters of baptism are very deep and mark us forever for a life of faith. Every time we come to the table and eat the bread and drink from the cup, we leave affirming our faith, renewed again for living in a world that needs Christians to work for justice and peace for all of God's people.

"Come unto me!" Simple words of welcome—simple, yet life changing for individuals and congregations!

Notes

1 Faith Nurturing: Whose Responsibility?

1. Hulda Niebuhr, "This and That," a collection of unpublished poetry (December 1929), Archives of the Jesuit-Krauss-McCormick Library, McCormick Theological Seminary, Chicago. Reprinted by permission of the estate of Hulda Niebuhr.

2. I am grateful to Jack Stotts for sharing this metaphor of "introducing dissonance into the familiar" in a convocation address he gave at McCormick Theological Seminary, September 1991.

3. Janet Fishburn, *Confronting the Idolatry of the Family: A New Vision for the Household of God* (Nashville: Abingdon Press, 1991), 34.

4. Ibid., 39.

5. Ibid., 145.

6. Letty Russell, *Household of Freedom: Authority in Feminist Theology* (Louisville: Westminster Press, 1987), 64–67.

7. Mary E. Hunt, "The Challenge of 'Both/And' Theology," in *Women and Church: The Challenge of Ecumenical Solidarity in an Age of Alienation,* ed. Melanie A. May (Grand Rapids, Mich.: Wm. B. Eerdmans, 1991), 29.

8. Robert Coles, *The Spiritual Life of Children* (Boston: Houghton Mifflin, 1990), xvi.

2 Pouring the Water

1. Gail Ramshaw, "Celebrating Baptism in Stages: A Proposal," in *Alternative Futures for Worship,* vol. 2 of *Baptism and Confirmation,* ed. Mark Searle (Collegeville, Minn.: Liturgical Press, 1987), 139.

2. Fishburn, *Confronting the Idolatry of Family,* 50.

3. My sister-in-law, Lyn Evans Caldwell, made a baptism book for our nephews on the occasion of their baptism. This affirmation is included in the book.

4. John Burkhart, *Worship* (Louisville: Westminster John Knox, 1982), 138–40.

5. Mark Searle, "Infant Baptism Reconsidered," in *Alternative Futures for Worship*, vol. 2 of *Baptism and Confirmation* (Collegeville, Minn.: Liturgical Press, 1987), 43.

6. *Book of Worship* (United Church of Christ, 1986)

7. *The Book of Order* (Presbyterian Church [U.S.A.], 1995).

8. Robert L. Browning and Roy A. Reed, *Models of Confirmation and Baptismal Affirmation* (Birmingham, Ala.: Religious Education Press, 1995), 116.

9. Fishburn, *Confronting the Idolatry of Family*, 136.

10. Robert L. Browning and Roy A. Reed, *The Sacraments in Religious Education and Liturgy* (Birmingham, Ala.: Religious Education Press, 1985), 141.

11. "Baptism, Eucharist, and Ministry," Faith and Order Paper no. 111 (Geneva: World Council of Churches, 1982), 2, 3.

12. Jeanne S. Fogle, *Signs of God's Love: Baptism and Communion* (Philadelphia: Geneva Press, 1984), 11.

13. Burkhart, *Worship*, 134.

14. There is much discussion about the trinitarian language used in baptisms. Many prefer the traditional wording of "Father, Son and Holy Spirit." Others search for language for God that is faithful to tradition yet inclusive. I am grateful to my colleague in ministry, Reverend Deborah Block, for sharing these words for God, which she uses at baptisms.

15. *The Book of Common Worship* (Presbyterian Church [U.S.A.], 1993), 406.

16. *Book of Worship*, 139.

17. Searle, "Infant Baptism Reconsidered," 44–45.

18. Louis H. Gunnemann, "Baptism—Sacrament of Christian Vocation," in "On the Way," vol. 3, no. 2 (occasional papers of the Wisconsin Conference of the United Church of Christ, winter 1985–86), 13.

19. Ibid., 18.

20. Ibid.

21. The title for this story is taken from an African proverb: "It takes a village to raise a child."

22. This model of celebrating baptism in stages was originally proposed by Gail Ramshaw-Schmidt in her chapter "Celebrating Baptism in Stages: A Proposal," in *Alternative Futures for Worship*, vol. 2 of *Baptism and Confirmation*, ed. Mark Searle (Collegeville, Minn.: Liturgical Press, 1987).

23. Brian Wren, "In Water We Grow," in *The Presbyterian Hymnal* (Louisville: Westminster John Knox, 1990).

24. Searle, "Infant Baptism Reconsidered," 44.

25. Robert Coles, *The Spiritual Life of Children* (Boston: Houghton Mifflin, 1990), 326.

26. Ibid., 326, 335.

3   Living in Response to Our Baptism

1. Fishburn, *Confronting the Idolatry of Family,* 49.

2. Ibid., 121.

3. Ibid., 122.

4. The concept of parenting for faith expression was suggested to me by a former student in a paper she wrote for one of my classes. I am grateful to Reverend Nancy H. Enderle for discussing this concept with me and suggesting I use it in a book such as this.

5. Sara Little, *To Set One's Heart: Belief and Teaching in the Church* (Louisville: John Knox Press, 1983), 17.

6. C. Ellis Nelson, *Where Faith Begins* (Louisville: John Knox Press, 1967), 10.

7. Little, *To Set One's Heart,* 18–21.

8. "Growing in the Life of the Christian Faith" (a study document of the Presbyterian Church [U.S.A.], 1991), 7.

9. Harold S. Kushner, *When Children Ask about God* (New York: Schocken Books, 1989), xiv.

10. Rabbi Marc Gellman and Monsignor Thomas Hartman, *Where Does God Live?* (New York: Triumph Books, 1991), 19–21.

11. John Westerhoff, *Bringing Up Children in the Christian Faith* (Minneapolis: Winston Press, 1980), 36.

12. Brian Wren, "Lord When You Came to Jordan," in *The Presbyterian Hymnbook* (Louisville: Westminster John Knox, 1990), 71.

13. Leontine T. C. Kelly, "Living Our Your Baptism: Baptism as Christian Vocation—An Ecumenical Perspective," *Reformed Liturgy and Music* 29, no. 1 (1995): 34.

14. I am indebted to my colleague Deborah Mullen for helping me understand the place of these renunciations within the baptismal liturgy. The discussion of her paper "Baptism: Sacrament of Struggle and Rite of Resistance" at a McCormick Theological Seminary faculty seminar has given me many insights.

15. J. Frederick Holper, "Choose This Day Whom You Will Serve: The Significance of Renunciations in the Sacrament of Baptism," *Reformed Liturgy and Music* 29, no. 2 (1995): 76.

16. *The Book of Common Worship,* 407.

17. Stanley Hauerwas and Brett Webb-Mitchell, "The Radical Edge of Baptism," *Reformed Liturgy and Music* 29, no. 2 (1995): 72.

18. Ibid., 73.

4   Setting the Table

1. Thanks to Reverend JoAnne Bogart for sharing this story during the annual meeting of the Rocky Mountain Conference of the United Church of Christ (May 1992).

2. John Burkhart, *Worship* (Louisville: Westminster Press, 1982), 137.

3. Ibid.

4. Catherine Gunsalus Gonsalez, *A Theology of the Lord's Supper* (Louisville: Presbyterian Church, 1981), 13.

5. Ibid.

6. "Statement of Faith" (United Church of Christ, 1981).

7. *Book of Worship,* 32.

8. *The Book of Order,* W-2.4006.

9. Betty Crowell, *Communion with Your Child* (paper delivered at the Connecticut Conference of the United Church of Christ, 1992), 3.

10. "Baptism, Eucharist, and Ministry," 10.

11. Ibid.

12. These words are used at the congregation where I worship, Lincoln Park Presbyterian Church in Chicago, just prior to coming to the table.

13. "Baptism, Eucharist, and Ministry," 11.

14. *The Book of Common Worship*, 145.

15. "Baptism, Eucharist, and Ministry," 13,

16. Ibid., 15.

17. Crowell, "Communion with Your Child," 4.

18. These questions are adapted from the book *God's Family at the Table: A Book for Parents and Children* by Virginia and Davis Thomas (Louisville: Presbyterian Church, 1981).

19. Leonardo Boff, *Sacraments of Life, Life of Sacraments* (Washington, D.C.: Pastoral Press, 1987), 32.

5   Moving from the Table

1. William Willimon, *Sunday Dinner: The Lord's Supper and the Christian Life* (Nashville: Upper Room, 1981), 95.

2. Ibid., 107.

3. Ellen T. Charry, "Raising Christian Children in a Pagan Culture," *Christian Century* (16 February 1994): 166.

4. Ibid.

5. John Burkhart discusses this meaning of communion in his book *Worship*, 92.

6. Willimon, *Sunday Dinner*, 100.

7. Fred Kaan (words) and Doreen Potter (music), "Let Us Talents and Tongues Employ" (Carol Stream, Ill.: Hope Publishing Company, 1975).

8. I am grateful to my friends and colleagues John Burkhart and Ruth Duck for first introducing me to the theological themes present in the eucharistic prayer, especially the last theme of the sacrament as rehearsal.

9. Ruth C. Duck, *Finding Words for Worship* (Louisville: Westminster John Knox, 1995), 90.

10. Fishburn, *Confronting the Idolatry of Family*, 137.

11. Ibid., 136–37.

12. Duck, *Finding Words for Worship*, 91.

13. Charry, "Raising Christian Children," 167.

14. Ibid.

15. Duck, *Finding Words for Worship*, 91.

16. Richard Foster, *Prayer: Finding the Heart's True Home* (San Francisco: Harper San Francisco, 1992), 7.

17. These figures from the Search Institutes study of effective Christian education were reported in Eugene C. Roehlkepartain, *The Teaching Church* (Nashville: Abingdon Press, 1993), 170.

18. Elsa Támez, "A Call to Commitment," from the *International Review of Mission*, October 1982 (p. 509), World Council of Churches, Geneva, Switzerland. Used with permission.

19. Rubem Alves, "A Common Longing," in *Sharing One Bread, Sharing One Mission: The Eucharist as Missionary Event*, ed. Jean Stromberg (Geneva: World Council of Churches, 1983), 7.

6   A Sacramental Model of Education in the Church

1. The shared praxis model is explained in Thomas Groome, *Christian Religious Education* (San Francisco: Harper and Row, 1980).

2. Roderick Kiracofe, *Cloth and Comfort: Pieces of Women's Lives from Their Quilts and Diaries* (New York: Clarkson Potter Publishers, 1994), 9.

3. Ibid., 57.

4. Ibid., 23, 41.

5. Thanks to Reverend Deborah Block for sharing this story. She is co-pastor of Immanuel Presbyterian Church in Milwaukee, Wisconsin.

6. Renae McKee-Parker, "Being Renewed: The Face of My Faith," unpublished poem (1995). Reprinted by permission of the author.

7. Renae McKee-Parker, letter to author, 20 August 1995.

8. Thanks to Reverend Mark Hindman for this story. He is pastor of Lake Bluff Community Church in Lake Bluff, Illinois.

9. Thanks to Reverend Nona Holy for this story. She is associate pastor of Parma South Presbyterian Church in Cleveland, Ohio, where she has major responsibility for programs of congregational nurture.

10. Thanks to Reverend Tracy Hindman of the First Presbyterian Church in Lake Forest, Illinois, for this story. She works with Donna Birney, a church elder, in designing and teaching the confirmation class program.

11. Thanks to Reverend John Wilkinson for this story. He is associate minister at the Fourth Presbyterian Church in Chicago.

Selected Bibliography

These books have been selected from the text as basic additions for a church library in the area of worship, education, and the sacraments.

"Baptism, Eucharist, and Ministry." Faith and Order Paper no. 111. Geneva: World Council of Churches, 1982.

Browning, Robert L., and Roy A. Reed. *Models of Confirmation and Baptismal Affirmation*. Birmingham, Ala.: Religious Education Press, 1995.

Burkhart, John. *Worship*. Louisville: Westminster John Knox, 1982.

Coles, Robert. *The Spiritual Life of Children*. Boston: Houghton Mifflin, 1990.

Cowen-Fletcher, Jane. *It Takes a Village*. New York: Scholastic Books, 1994.

Duck, Ruth. *Finding Words for Worship*. Louisville: Westminster John Knox, 1995.

Duckert, Mary. *New Kid in the Pew*. Louisville: Westminster John Knox, 1991.

Fogle, Jeanne S. *Signs of God's Love: Baptism and Communion*. Philadelphia: Geneva Press, 1984.

Gellman, Marc, and Thomas Hartman. *How Do You Spell God? Answers to the Big Questions from Around the World*. New York: Morrow Junior Books, 1995.

Harris, Maria. *Fashion Me a People: Curriculum in the Church*. Louisville: Westminster John Knox, 1989.

Ramshaw, Gail. *Sunday Morning*. Chicago: Liturgy Training Publications, 1993.

Russell, Letty. *Household of Freedom: Authority in Feminist Theology*. Louisville: Westminster Press, 1987.

Sandell, Elizabeth J. *Including Children in Worship: A Planning Guide for Congregations*. Minneapolis: Augsburg, 1991.

Sasso, Sandy Eisenberg. *In God's Name*. Woodstock, Vt.: Jewish Lights Publishing, 1994.

Searle, Mark, ed. *Alternative Futures for Worship*. Vol. 2, *Baptism and Confirmation*. Collegeville, Minn: Liturgical Press, 1987.

Westerhoff, John. *Bringing Up Children in the Christian Faith*. Minneapolis: Winston Press, 1980.